MAKING PARTNER

The Essential Guide to Negotiating the Law School Path and Beyond

ADAM GROPPER

Printed in the United States of America.

17 16 15 14 13   5 4 3 2 1

Library of Congress Cataloging-in-Publication Data is on file.

ISBN 978-1-62722-259-4

CONTENTS

ACKNOWLEDGMENTS

There are several people that helped make this project possible and I am pleased to have the opportunity to acknowledge them here.

Thank you to my former law firm mentors, Henry, Roger, David, and Rob, whose preferences, mannerisms, and teachings are referred to in the book and who together trained me how to talk, think, and write like a lawyer while sharing a few pointers about tax practice, hospitality law, and the business of law generally. I feel very honored to have had the opportunity to be mentored by people of such personal character and professional caliber.

Thank you to my wife and best friend, Amy, who selflessly provided unending patience, support, and encouragement throughout this entire process, from the first drafts to publication. Amy's insightful feedback and helpful comments on style and substance greatly enhanced the content and quality of this book. I feel quite lucky to be connected to such a giving, kind-hearted person and companion.

Thank you to my toddler daughter Emma, whose good nature, playful personality, and regular sleep schedule helps to make fatherhood look easy and allowed me the necessary time to place the finishing touches on this book. I am so proud to be the parent of such a special and talented girl.

Thank you to my mom who helped fuel my ambition, encouraged me to become a lawyer, and perhaps most relevant to this book, taught me the value of persistence and not giving up. Mom's valuable advice and encouragement to go after the brass ring helped me through all my rejections and ultimately put me in this position where I could offer instructions to others about how to do the same. I feel grateful to be the son of such an amazing and strong woman.

Thank you to my in-laws, Gigi and Rob, for their support and interest in talking about the book and offering useful suggestions along the way. I feel privileged to have such decent, caring people in my life.

Thank you to my friends for sharing in my excitement for this project. I appreciate all of them.

Thank you to my publisher, Rick, for recognizing the value of this project from the beginning and helping see to it that the book was published. It has been a pleasure to work with him.

ABOUT THE AUTHOR

Adam Gropper is the founder of www.legaljob.com, a blog providing practical advice for law students and law firm associates. The blog focuses on guidance for maximizing performance in school, securing the dream job, excelling as an associate, and moving on the fast track to making partner. Mr. Gropper regularly participates on panels to discuss these topics at several law schools and at events organized by various bar associations. He also frequently meets with and serves as a mentor to George Washington University law students and other law students and law firm associates who seek career advice.

Mr. Gropper is a Legislation Counsel on the staff of the non-partisan Congressional Joint Committee on Taxation, assisting Members of both parties in Congress in developing and drafting tax legislation and legislative history with a focus on the area of tax procedure and administration. Previously, Mr. Gropper was a tax partner at Baker & Hostetler LLP ("Baker") where he spent ten years handling tax controversy and planning matters. At Baker, he achieved favorable results for clients at audit, in IRS Appeals, and in tax litigation and provided domestic and international tax planning support for clients, including preparing formal written tax advice, opinions, and IRS ruling requests.

Mr. Gropper is a licensed Certified Public Accountant and has a Juris Doctor, with honors, from the George Washington University Law School, a Master of Taxation from Florida Atlantic University, and a Bachelor of Science in Accounting, with honors, from the University of Florida.

INTRODUCTION

This book provides practical information and specific advice about how to obtain a position at a top law firm of any size, including AmLaw 100 firms,[1] and how to excel once you are there. The advice is given in the form of a step-by-step explanation of a highly effective and proven method used to secure a top law firm job,[2] and detailed best practices to follow to be a star associate on the fast track to partnership and a successful junior partner.

This book is recommended for anyone considering law school and for law students at every level of their law school careers: during law school and the summer after law school. First-year law students (1Ls), for example, may find it useful as they scramble for their summer jobs. Concurrently, upper-level students may find it useful in tailoring their permanent job searches.

This book is also recommended for medium and large law firm associates at all levels. For instance, first-year associates may find it useful as they seek to make a strong first impression on senior associates and partners. At the same time, mid-level associates may find it useful for providing guidance regarding their transition from junior associate.

Although this book focuses on law, the steps for securing a top job and succeeding once there could also be helpful in other fields. The principles in this book can be used by people interested in working in any environment where the competition is tough and the jobs are limited, including in

---

1. The term *AmLaw 100 firm* refers to one of the top 100 law firms in the country by gross revenues. *American Lawyer* magazine surveys these firms every year, and its AmLaw 100 survey is well known and respected. As part of its survey, *American Lawyer* also ranks these 100 firms by various profit indicators, including profits per partner and revenue per lawyer.
2. Note that if the goal is to work at a top law firm, the focus in law school should still be on earning top grades and trying to secure a position through the traditional fall interviewing program. Accordingly, the guidance provided here should be seen as a supplement to this traditional approach, and there is no guarantee that a top law firm job will be obtained using the alternative approaches presented. Moreover, not everyone will be comfortable pursuing a law firm job in the manner discussed.

industry, and at accounting and consulting firms.

Given the current law market and the considerable expense of law school, it may be worthwhile to spend some time thinking about whether you plan to practice as a lawyer after law school. If the answer is no, it may still make sense to go (after weighing the cost, including the opportunity cost) because learning how to reason like a lawyer seems to be a helpful skill for any profession, as evidenced by the many successful JDs in areas outside the law (and the various books that provide information about different careers possible for JDs). If the answer is yes and the plan (at least for now) is specifically to practice at a top firm, there are two schools of thought about how your choice of law school can best help you achieve this goal.

First, it is widely recognized that having a degree and excellent grades from a top-20 law school places you in the best possible position to secure a top law firm position. Short of that preferred path, the question is whether to attend a highly ranked law school or go to a less prestigious law school and have a better shot at being at the top of the class. The conventional wisdom has been to go to the most highly ranked law school possible. This notion has been challenged recently by two law school professors, who suggest that performance in law school is more important than law school "eliteness." Thus, in their view, you can increase your top law firm prospects by doing well at a lower ranked school versus being in the middle of the pack of a higher ranked school. Richard Sander & Jane Bambauer, *The Secret of My Success: How Status, Eliteness, and School Performance Shape Legal Careers*, 9 JOURNAL OF EMPIRICAL LEGAL STUDIES 4, 893–930 (2012). Both sides have merit and should be evaluated. To help break the impasse (and consistent with the advice provided here), consider attending the law school that potentially can benefit you most in terms of exposing you to the area(s) of law in which you may want to practice (understanding and assuming the risk that your original preferences may change). To determine the school best matched to your preferences, weigh your responses to these forward-thinking questions: Is the law school known for the specialty you are thinking about? Does the school offer many courses in that specialty? Is there an option to obtain a certificate in that specialty? Is there a professor at the law school who is nationally recognized in that area? Does the law school offer a clinic or other opportunity to practice that area of law during school for credit? Is the school in a location where there are lots of employment opportunities for your specialty (i.e., Washington, D.C., for a regulatory niche such as tax or securities law)? A majority of yes answers to these questions indicates that the law school is a strong match to your current preferences, and the exposure the school provides you to your specialty should prove helpful for securing a position at a top law firm.

This book demonstrates what may be possible for those willing to invest the extensive effort and time to complete the steps discussed herein and for those who will not be deterred by constant rejection. I was inspired to write this book and help others after being turned down by hundreds of firms, including two rejections from the law firm that ended up hiring me and eventually admitting me as partner.

This information should be extremely helpful at various times in your law career, especially for readers who come from a family that does not have a law background or experience getting into and working at a top firm. First, it will help you to have this information early in law school so that as law students, you can follow the GPS: Get good grades early, Pick a major, and Specialize (by gaining academic and work experience in a niche area) as soon as practically possible. Next, this advice will be valuable when trying to get a job. Law students can learn how to take a DIP (and get into a top law firm) as they Distinguish themselves, Interview with people who care, and Practice persistence. Once onboard at the firm, associates will find the book advantageous as a reference for best practices such as how to determine partner preferences and satisfy them, be rigorous, and manage workload effectively to ensure success as a junior and mid-level associate. This advice will come in handy especially at those crucial times in your associate career when you may have the option to switch firms and prove yourself all over again. It will also be useful to consult as a senior associate on the road to partner, so that you are prepared to learn the business of practicing law and are in the best possible position to make partner when first eligible. Finally, the guidance, if followed, will help ensure a smooth transition from star associate to successful junior partner as you manage current clients effectively, network strategically, seek referrals, and continue to build your brand.

This book also comes at an important time. Data show that the legal job market has still not recovered from the 2008 recession. For example, only 56 percent of 2012 law graduates were employed in permanent full-time jobs requiring a law degree within nine months of graduation (the standard measuring period).[3] The overall 2012 employment rate after nine months was higher: it was 84.7 percent, according to data gathered by the National Association of Law Placement, but even that figure was the lowest since 1994.[4]

Accordingly, many current law students are worried with good reason about the prospect of securing a top law firm job during this currently down job market. Similarly, many law graduates at top law firms are anxious about keeping their jobs, much less making partner. Thus advice about securing an offer from a top law firm and excelling once there is sorely needed. Rigorous application of the advice provided in this book should greatly improve the chances of securing an offer from a top law firm and excelling once you are there. Job offers may be more competitive than in years past, but they are still out there, especially for people who are determined and willing to apply the effort necessary to make it happen.

This book is organized in six easy-to-read chapters, starting chronologically with law school and concluding with life as a junior partner at a top law firm. Chapter 1 discusses how to succeed in law school. Chapter 2 discusses how to determine whether to pursue a position at a top law firm. Chapter 3 discusses how to secure a top law firm position. Chapter 4 discusses how to succeed as an associate at a top law firm. Chapter 5 discusses how to make partner at a top law firm. Chapter 6 discusses how to succeed as a junior partner at a top law firm.

The material that follows should be able to be read quickly. The most important takeaway points (TAPs) are listed at the beginning of each chapter, followed by detailed suggestions for applying the TAPs. The six TAPs are as follows: (1) To succeed in law school, follow the GPS: Get good grades early, Pick a law major, and Specialize. (2) To help determine whether to pursue a top law firm position, ask yourself if you are comfortable being a salesman. (3) To get into a top law firm, take a DIP: Distinguish yourself, Interview with people who care, and Practice persistence. (4) To become a top-performing associate, follow these soft skill practices: determine and

---

3. The complete 2012 Employment Summary Report, including data for individual schools, is available at http://employmentsummary.abaquestionnaire.org/ (last visited August 12, 2013).

4. National Association for Law Placement (NALP), Press Release. Law School Class of 2012 Finds More Jobs Starting Salaries Rise—But Large Class Size Hurts Overall Employment Rate (June 20, 2013), available at http://www.nalp.org/uploads/PressReleases/Classof2012SelectedFindinPressRelease_june2013.pdf (last visited August 12, 2013) (The overall employment rate fell from 85.6 percent in 2011 and the rate has now fallen for five years since 2018. The overall employment rate was also at 84.7 percent in 1994.).

satisfy partner preferences, be rigorous, manage workload effectively, seek specific feedback and take action, make others look good, document performance results annually, have a partner's mind-set, and secure an effective sponsor. (5) To become a partner, stay productive, be active inside and outside the firm, serve in firm leadership roles, demonstrate that you care about the business of practicing law, become an expert, consider secondment opportunities, and make your case. (6) To succeed as a junior partner, manage current clients effectively, network strategically, seek referrals, take the long view, and continue to build your brand and distinguish yourself.

I hope the information provided in this book is helpful in your pursuit of a position at a top law firm and along your road to partner.

Good luck!

CHAPTER 1
How to Be Successful in Law School

TAP 1: To succeed in law school, follow the GPS:

1. Get good grades early.
2. Pick a law "major."
3. Specialize (by gaining academic and work experience in a niche area).

The law school program for helping place students at law firms generally requires law students to interview after they complete the first law school (1L) year. To maximize your opportunities through this program, it is helpful to earn good grades early, hence step 1. In addition, law firms (and other employers) are interested in hiring law students who have demonstrated a pattern of interest in the particular practice area for which they are interviewing. This commitment can be shown by taking and excelling in classes focusing on a particular practice of law—and, if possible, a niche area within that practice—and by obtaining relevant work experience, hence steps 2 and 3. Note that steps 2 and 3, pick a major and specialize, do not necessarily follow each other. You may pick a law "major" or decide to change your major only after concentrating on a niche within a particular practice area.

STEP 1: GET GOOD GRADES EARLY
Step 1 seems obvious, but it is so important that it deserves mention up front. Grades should be your first, second, and third priority because earning excellent grades will open up plenty of opportunities for legal jobs, particularly at the big firms. It will be much easier to sell yourself to future employers by showing them your transcript with straight As and not hav-

ing to explain why your transcript should be looked at in the context of all your experience and grades in classes that are relevant to your practice area. Thus, it is a good idea to keep outside activities (whatever the opportunity, generally) to a minimum early in law school, because they will likely interfere with studying or other time you may need to perform your best. This advice may seem inconsistent with the guidance given later, which discusses the importance of securing relevant work experience while in law school. Both are important, however; they are just a matter of priorities, which can change at different times in your law school career. Earning good grades should be the focus, especially as a 1L. As a 2L and 3L, gaining valuable work or academic experience in a niche area may become the priority, particularly if you are still seeking a top law firm position.

Why Early?

Put simply: peak early, if possible. The time to shine is in your first year. Obviously, everyone would like to do well in law school. But if you are one who lacks the staying power and momentum to give it your all throughout your time in law school, then concentrate on hitting it out of the park your first year.

The bottom line is that students who excel their first year put themselves in the best possible position to secure employment as a summer associate at a top law firm after their second year of law school and ultimately to secure a full-time position at that firm.

First-year grades are the most important because potential top law firm employers (and other employers) make decisions about granting interviews and hiring law students for summer associate positions in the fall semester of the second year. Thus their decision is generally based only on the results of the two semesters of the first year.

Accordingly, the idea is to earn top grades your first year and make Law Review (the journal whose admission is reserved for the top 10 percent of the class). This pattern will provide you with the greatest number of top law firm choices for the fall recruitment process. Once at the firm, most summer associates are generally granted an offer to start in the fall after graduation and the bar exam (regardless of whether that candidate earns poor or average grades in their second and third years). Given the current economy, in some circumstances, full-time hiring decisions may be made only after considering second- and third-year performance. Also, some top-level law firms may still be deferring start dates (or withdrawing acceptances) because of the impact the recession is having on clients (and therefore the amount of legal work available).[1] Still, it is fair to say that students who excel in their first year put themselves in the best possible position to secure top law firm jobs.

So what happens if you do not earn great grades as a 1L? Should you give up on securing a job at a top law firm? No! You may face a more difficult path, but by following the steps discussed in this book, including picking a major and specializing by gaining experience (both covered in this chapter), you can put yourself in a strong position to overcome this setback.[2]

How?

The following two practices are commonly cited by professors and successful law students for earning top grades.

Review Previous Exams and Join a Study Group

Generally, law students who earn good grades early seem to take the following two action steps: (1) review previous exams; and (2) join a study group comprised of dedicated, bright students (or, at a minimum, students who work hard and achieve strong results).

Previous exams are helpful because the style of questioning and even the major areas targeted tend not to change too much over time, even if the specific questions are different. Reviewing the exams at the beginning of the semester (as well as before exam time) will likely help you get a feel for each professor's thinking process early on and the areas they think are important

---

1. According to one AmLaw 100 firm partner, "like many other firms, we have these deferral programs ... where we encouraged students to go out for a year or so and do something else at a fraction of their salary." NALP & The NALP Foundation, *A Roundtable on the Future of Lawyer Hiring, Development and Advancement—Adjusting to the New Normal* (April 11, 2011), 21–22, available at http://www. nclp.org/uploads/documents/April11RoundtableFinalTranscript0419.pdf(last visited August 13, 2013), [hereinafter "NALP April 2011 Roundtable"].

2. Law school career development counselors generally advise that if you do not receive an offer from a big firm during the fall interviewing process, it may make sense to focus your efforts on employers other than large firms and large government agencies.

We've had to spend a lot more time educating students that although large firms and government agencies—larger government agencies—may recruit in [the fall interviewing program] and have the ability to recruit earlier in the process, there's still a lot of other employers that may not know their needs until the spring of their 2L year, and that you have to prepare and lay the foundation and network and really try to get yourself involved with those employers as soon as you can, knowing the process is probably going to take a lot longer.

NALP & The NALP Foundation, *A Roundtable on the Future of Lawyer Hiring, Development and Advancement—Adjusting to the New Normal* (June 8, 2011), 16, available at http:// www.nalp.org/june8futureoflawyerhiring (last visited July 9, 2013) [hereinafter "NALP June 2011 Roundtable"].

Notwithstanding this advice, this book provides tools that should help you continue to focus on big firm opportunities despite a poor showing in the fall program.

to emphasize.

Study groups can be helpful because they expose you to different patterns of thought and multiple ways to approach the same legal question. Given that most law school exams are highly subjective, exposure to smart people with different perspectives can be helpful for learning how to think and for anticipating the types of questions likely to be asked. By exam time, study group participants likely will have an edge over students not in study groups or those who chose to study with friends who may not be as strongly motivated or who may be at lower intelligence levels.

The next section discusses the second step every law student should take.

STEP 2: PICK A LAW "MAJOR"

Why?

A great way to differentiate yourself from your law school classmates (besides getting good grades early) is to pick a major. That is, to decide (as early as realistically possible, after performing the necessary due diligence) what broad area of law you want to spend your time thinking and learning about.

There is no formal declaration of a major in law school, but you can do so internally by taking more than one or two classes in that area or an area that is relevant (as a 2L and a 3L) and by obtaining substantive work experience in that area. One big decision is whether your focus will be on an area of law that is so-called code-based. Very generally, if your major is code-based, for example, you have decided to focus on Title 26 of the United States Code (U.S.C.) for tax law, Title 15 for Indian law, or Title 17 for copyright law. If constitutional law interests you, your focus will be the U.S. Constitution rather than the U.S.C. This explanation is somewhat simplistic because the U.S.C. or the Constitution will be far from your only source for the particular practice area, although the primary one.

It is important to pick a major because employers (who want to mitigate their risk that you will not work out) generally prefer to hire someone who has shown strong interest and commitment to a particular practice area.

Easier said than done, right? If you are like many law school students, you probably are not sufficiently informed about the universe of choices available to pick from both in terms of legal settings and practice areas.

Where Do You Start?

Law students generally come into law school with at best a limited idea about what it means to practice law. They have even less knowledge about the variety of settings in which particular areas can be practiced.

One place it may be helpful to start is to think about the settings where you would want to work. For some possible reasons why you may want to work at a top firm, consider the following excerpts from associates at top law firms who secured their jobs in a nontraditional manner (i.e., outside the fall interviewing program). Their comments about how they secured their jobs are provided later in Chapter 3.

"I wanted to work for a top law firm because I believe it is the most exciting and challenging career option available to law students. Working for a top law firm means working with attorneys who are at the top of their profession and counseling clients who are leaders in their respective industries. I have always been very ambitious and, for me, a top law firm position was the natural position for which to aim. I do not think I would have been satisfied with any other type of position. The fact that top law firm jobs are well compensated definitely adds to their appeal, but the money is not the primary reason I wanted to work for such a firm."

"Primarily financial and prestige. I wanted to move to Miami and wanted to work for the best firm in the city that would give me the greatest opportunities to advance my career and to compensate me at or near the top of the market in that city."

"There were two primary reasons. First, upon completion of law school I had a family of four (with a fifth on the way) to support. My fifth was born while I was studying for the bar! I was interested in the most financially rewarding position I could land.

"Equally, if not more important, however, was the desire to excel in a specialty that I had an affinity and aptitude for. A position in a non-top law firm would, almost invariably, not have afforded me the high quality, intellectually stimulating and challenging work, that I desperately desired and happily acquired in the job I landed with a top 100 law firm."

"Top law firms provide me with the opportunity to work on cross border transactions involving complex tax issues and the opportunity to work with attorneys who are specialized in specific tax areas."

"The number one reason I wanted to work at a top law firm was financial. I also sought to work at a top law firm because I hoped to work on interesting cases that would capture my attention and with intelligent attorneys who would help develop my skills."

Knowing your preferences will help you determine the type of lawyer you would want to be before narrowing in on a practice area. To get you thinking along these lines, consider the following examples. You could be a (1) firm (of varying size) civil practice lawyer; (2) firm (of varying size) criminal defense lawyer; (3) sole practitioner; (4) prosecutor or public defender; (5) noncriminal government agency lawyer; (6) public-interest lawyer; (7) in-house counsel, or (8) clerk for a judge.

To aid in your decision about the environment in which you would want to practice (and thereby the type of lawyer you would want to be), consider gathering the following types of information about each job category: (1) a general description; (2) salary averages; (3) average weekly work hours; (4) potential for advancement; (5) common credentials/qualifications hirers in the area expect; (6) pros and cons of the job; (7) accounts of what job holders do in a typical day; and (8) job satisfaction levels. Is there a particular type of lawyer from the previous list for which the responses satisfy most of your preferences?

Once you have a general idea of what type of lawyer and where you would work, you can apply those preferences to a particular specialty area of the law. Fortunately, there are some resources available to help. For example, the University of Michigan Law School Office of Career Services has developed a practice area chart to provide an overview of the various legal settings for the top 25 practice areas.[3]

Let's assume you have followed this approach and decide you may be interested in exploring the practice area of tax law. Following the pattern outlined earlier, first you would have considered different legal settings in-

---

3. *Top 25 Practice Areas and Sample Practice Settings,* University of Michigan Law School Office of Career Services and the Office of Public Service (June 2010), available at http://www.law.umich.edu/careers/practicearea/Documents/practicesettings.pdf (last visited July 9, 2013).

cluding the private sector, government, or nonprofit world. Applying these settings to the practice area of tax translates to private sector opportunities in a law firm (small, boutique, or large), a consulting firm, an accounting firm, and in-house (private or public corporations, banks, etc.). In government, a tax lawyer can work for the (1) executive branch of the federal government in the Department of the Treasury, the Internal Revenue Service (IRS), the Department of Justice: Tax Division (both criminal and civil), and U.S. Attorneys' Offices; (2) legislative branch as a staffer for a Member of Congress or congressional committee, including Finance, Ways and Means, and Joint Committee on Taxation; and (3) judicial branch as a clerk for the U.S. Tax Court, the U.S. Court of Federal Claims, and state tax courts. A tax lawyer can also work for state governments at state tax authorities. In the nonprofit sector, a tax lawyer can work for nonprofit charities that advocate on behalf of low-income taxpayers, low-income tax clinics, poverty law groups, large public entities such as hospitals and foundations, and large charities.

To learn more about the different practice areas available, including the skills and training required and narratives from practitioners about their daily work life, it may be helpful to review the *Official Guide to Legal Specialties: An Insider's Guide to Every Major Practice Area* (2000, published for the National Association for Law Placement by Barbri Group), by Lisa L. Abrams, J.D. That book provides a sense of life as a lawyer practicing a particular area of the law, including the types of matters such lawyers handle, the different environments in which that area is practiced, and the type of clients handled.

You can build on all this information you have gathered through the networking tips discussed below. However, this preliminary research should be enough to at least get you started on narrowing down the environments and practice area.

How Do You Choose a Major?

How can you pick a major without knowing what lawyers in different practice areas actually do, or without having any real idea what area of law you might enjoy practicing? After all, many law students are in law school because they could not decide on a career path in college. So, how is that going to change now?

For one thing, you will have reviewed resources that can provide you a big picture of the categories available and how the major practice areas line up with those categories. Armed with this information, take every opportunity (attend school and career events, talk with family and friends, perform your own networking efforts, etc.), to find out how someone ended up in the legal field where they are practicing. The answer to this question may help you in your search for a legal career path. It does not matter if a person works in a legal area about which you are not interested. It is the thought and action process of knowing how the person ended up in that area that may help you as you begin to evaluate different possibilities.

Three specific steps you can take to help get you started in choosing a major (after considering the different settings where law is practiced, the characteristics of those settings, and your preferences) are: (1) think hard; (2) network with a plan; and (3) decide as soon as feasible.

Think Hard

It seems obvious, but set aside some serious time to consider what you like to think about. What are your hobbies? What types of books and magazines appeal to you? What things are you particularly a natural at doing? If you do not know, your friends and family probably have some thoughts. Remember also the tons of books out there that purport to help you discover what makes you tick.

It is nice if you can eventually match your interest to an area where demand for legal services happens to be high. You may not be able to; but if you have no clue about what major to choose, this step is worth doing. Use the career development office and other resources to help analyze which legal practice areas are booming. Regulatory areas likely always will be strong; in particular, consider areas where Congress has passed some major legislation recently (or will tinker with in the future)—tax, health care, intellectual property, securities law, and so forth.

There are at least four things to consider. It is helpful if your area (1) is one in which you have more than a passing interest; (2) matches your experience, education, or particular skill set (i.e., photographic memory is helpful in litigation and many other areas), or some combination of all three; (3) is considered a growth area (both now and in the foreseeable future); and (4) provides multiple possibilities for obtaining a job outside traditional routes.

An example of a specialty area that meets these criteria is tax law. The opportunities in tax law are strong; most practitioners are older and on the way to retirement, the tax law changes all the time, and these new laws add to its complexity. So, tax is a short- and long-term growth area. This high demand means that smart candidates with relevant experience or education (i.e., some evidence that they will be successful in the area) will have an opportunity to make their case (through effective networking and other tools discussed in this book) outside the traditional process of waiting for a job posting and submitting a resume. More detail on each of these considerations is provided below.

Have More than a Passing Interest

You should shoot for having more than a passing interest in the particular area you choose. The reason is straightforward: the stronger the interest level, the easier it will be to (1) work all of the hours required to satisfy clients (including partners) and become an expert in your niche area; (2) sell your services (to partners, colleagues, clients, other lawyers in the industry); and (3) distinguish yourself from the competition (including writing and speaking).

Match the Major to Your Background

Your major should match your relevant work experience, education, or particular skill set (e.g., proficiency in a different language). Possessing just one of these items may be enough to distinguish you from the competition. Employers look for commitment to the practice area. Experience, education, or demonstration of a particular skill set will help establish this commitment. One or more of these items may also help you to predict whether you will excel in the particular practice area.

It is also possible that some of you may have no academic and work experience in their chosen field until they decide to pursue that field. That situation is okay, and it does not mean that you should pick a different major. Once you do make the decision, however, you will want to get that experience to help demonstrate your commitment to the area, as discussed later.

Match Your Interest to a Booming Legal Field

Consider law fields where demand is high that also match your interests. Job security can come with picking a growth area. Ask some of these questions. What is the average age of most of the lawyers in this practice area? What is happening in the world (current events, Congress, courts, executive branch, agencies) that affects this practice area? What is the outlook in that area for the foreseeable future?

Identify Multiple Paths for Obtaining a Job

Consider that the narrower or more technical the area, the fewer the number of skilled practitioners. So employers may have to cast a wider net than usual to find their ideal candidate. In certain niche areas, law schools and overall grades still matter; but grades in the practice area and substantive experience are particularly important. Certain specialty areas (i.e., tax or health law) are growing and becoming more complicated every day, so the demand for more lawyers is rising and the supply may not match the demand by the time you graduate.

Network with a Plan

Ask the career development office to provide you with lists of people for which you have commonalities or so-called touchpoints. Some examples of touchpoints are same undergraduate school, same undergraduate major, same hometown, similar cultural background, and so on. One of the touchpoints could be an area of law you may be interested in; but you may not know that yet, so it is okay if that is not on the list. Contact 10–15 of these people for the purpose of finding out about how each of them ended up in the legal field in which they are practicing. Ask each person what it is like to practice in their particular area of law. State upfront that you are not looking for a job. Request a short meeting for coffee when and where it is most convenient for them. Be mindful of their time. The goal of each meeting is to get the name of another contact person they think would be helpful for you to meet.

Decide as Soon as Feasible

Do not be afraid to commit for fear of missing out on other areas. Know that you can and may change your major so the sooner you pick, the better. All is not lost if you spent a long time on the wrong major, because you may be able to transfer some or all of the skills and education to the new major.

The pitch to the employer is not so much about your liking this area versus that one, but that your skill set is more suitable for the current area for the following identifiable reasons . . . that help you think, talk, and write like a lawyer practicing this kind of law.

STEP 3: SPECIALIZE WITHIN THE MAJOR YOU PICKED

After picking your major, you can demonstrate your commitment and further distinguish yourself to potential employers by going one level deeper.

Choose to specialize, and pick a concentration within that major. Your major is the broad body of law within which you will operate, for example, tax, insurance, or intellectual property. Your concentration or niche answers the questions of who your clients are and what legal services you will provide them.

Within the tax "major," for example, you could decide to work in estate tax planning. This area involves representing clients and individuals and helping them plan ways to minimize their federal and state estate tax before death. Alternatively, you could decide to work in estate tax controversy, in which case you would represent estates under IRS audit.

It is important to realize that your choices may not occur in the order being described. Step 3, choosing to specialize and picking a concentration, may happen before step 2, choosing a broader major, because the niche area may appeal to you more readily than the major itself. To specialize within your major, start by taking—and excelling in—classes covering the broad major. Then continue by taking at least one class in the concentration area itself, if possible. In addition to classes, obtain substantive work experience focusing on that niche within the major, as discussed next.

Classes

Soon after you pick a major, it will be helpful to demonstrate some commitment to the practice area generally and a niche within the area specifically. Any sustained pattern could work. For example, you might take (and do well in) multiple law school classes in one subject area. You likely have to wait until you are a 2L before being able to choose your classes. At that point, nearly every course you take should be carefully chosen to target some potential employer or job type.

Before going forward with your "major" coursework, make sure that you are signing up for classes that genuinely interest you. If this is not the case, you may want to reconsider your major.

Obviously, the goal is to love what you ultimately end up doing. But in the short term, your task is much more strategic. The idea is to take classes that give you the strongest chance of succeeding so you can distinguish yourself from your peers and increase your marketability. If you are interested in something, you are more likely to perform well naturally and without much effort (or at least the effort will not seem like much, even if you are spending large amounts of time on the course). Accordingly, you may want to pick classes with the potential to move you if possible. This plan will not help you get good grades early (as discussed in step 1), but it may help you climb back up after a tough first year.

You will find that some majors are easier to demonstrate a commitment to, because law schools offer many classes in that subject area. Examples include intellectual property, tax, corporate law, family law, litigation, and health law. In these cases, you may want to consider taking courses that are directly on topic as well as some that complement the area. For example, if you want to specialize in corporate law, then you may want to take corporations, securities regulations, venture capital law, and takeovers but also consider complementary classes like corporate tax and bankruptcy. As another example, if you are interested in mergers and acquisitions (M&A) work, taking courses on corporations is a must, but you may be in a stronger position vis-à-vis your peers if you have also taken (and performed well in) securities law and takeovers. To get started, you may want to look at your school's job board and review job postings for 2Ls and 3Ls to determine what subjects would be considered complementary and perhaps provide you a leg up for those jobs. If you are fairly sure of your choice of major, you may want to consider picking two related majors. For example, tax and M&A work go hand in hand, as do intellectual property and litigation.

Job Experience

Another way to demonstrate commitment to (and confirm your interest in) a practice area (and, in particular, a niche within that area) is to gain some substantive work experience either in the summer or during school. Remember that during school you want to focus on obtaining the highest grades possible, so you may not want to divide your time with work, particularly in that crucial first year.

When evaluating potential job opportunities, one of the most important criteria to look for is which employer might allow you the opportunity to do heavy lifting. In other words, where can you get the most substantive experience and/or have input (direct or indirect) into the decision-making process? Where are you going to best be able to learn how to write, think, and talk like a lawyer? Where can you learn what it is truly like to practice your chosen area of law generally and the niche area specifically? The endgame is that you want to be in a position to explain your contributions concisely to a future employer and demonstrate how that particular experience makes you valuable to the prospective employer.[4]

Consider the following pros and cons for different types of potential summer or part-time work experiences. Very generally, working in a big firm has prestige, comes with a large paycheck, and offers the potential to work on sophisticated matters. However, you may find that working for a small boutique that specializes in a certain area of law provides you more opportunities to gain the type and amount of experience that will be valuable to a future employer.

Working for Congress, especially for a particular committee, could be rewarding if people there are working on major legislation that affects your concentration area. But again, confirm that you will be involved (at least somewhat; attending key meetings, for example) in all or major aspects of the process (in addition to the typical and useful research and memo writing). This same analysis can be done for a government agency. More information about securing relevant job experience is provided later, in Chapter 3.

Now that you have followed the GPS and made yourself an attractive candidate for a top law firm, you are ready to continue the sales process required to get into a top law firm. That's right, sales. It probably makes sense here to point out that succeeding at a top law firm (from getting in to making partner) requires sales skills, as discussed in Chapter 2.

---

4. Substantive experience will increase your chances of securing an AmLaw 100 firm position, as discussed in more detail later. According to one AmLaw 100 firm partner, for example, "[c]lients want fully trained associates. And they don't want to be paying to train an associate on their nickel." NALP April 2011 Roundtable, p. 9.

CHAPTER 2
How to Determine Whether to Pursue a Position at a Top Law Firm

TAP 2: To help determine whether to pursue a top law firm position, ask yourself if you are comfortable being a salesperson.

This chapter explains an idea that may not be readily apparent to law students. The idea is that effective sales skills are required in multiple stages of your law firm career, including getting into the firm, securing high-quality work from partners, promoting yourself in and outside the firm, and eventually making partner. That's right—you went to law school to be the best salesperson.

Accordingly, if you decide to go the law firm route, you will benefit from sharpening your sales skills. If you are not a salesperson and cannot bear to learn this craft even a little bit, you may want to consider whether life in a law firm is a match for you.

Many people decide to go to law school because they do not want to be a salesperson, so going to business school makes little sense. Preparing business plans, selling, marketing, reinventing yourself—none of these tasks is for them. They prefer the prestigious profession of law, where people spend their time thinking about the law and crafting cogent legal arguments. Unfortunately, the practice of law today is spent doing much more than that. So if you fall into this group, a government job or a position in-house at a major corporation might be more suitable for you.[1]

---

1. Undoubtedly, every job will involve some sales elements as you demonstrate to your client (whether it is the government, a company, an association, etc.) that you are competent. However, at the law firm, constant selling is required to be successful.

As discussed in the next chapter, salesmanship at a top law firm begins up front as you articulate how you have distinguished yourself from the competition (by following the guidance in Chapter 1) to obtain a coveted spot at the firm. Remember that these days, a strong resume does not necessarily speak for itself.

After proving yourself worthy of a position, you have a new sales task. Your job as a law firm associate is to prove to the partners that in addition to your intellect and competency, you can handle a variety of projects, be efficient, and produce solid work product every time. The rat race begins on day one, because you want to be the associate who is one of the go-to people for demanding partners. Having a full plate all the time is job security (at least in the short term) and helps when raise and promotion time come around.

The self-promoting continues as you rise in the firm. Even more self-promotion occurs then, because partners need an excuse to use you at your increasing billable rate versus a junior superstar with much lower rates. You may also try selling your ability to handle increasing responsibility on some accounts in the hopes that a senior partner will make you supervising lawyer on a case and eventually hand you the keys to the kingdom and make you the billing lawyer. Also, as you become more senior, you will no doubt have face time with various clients, which requires sales skills to be effective. You may have to convince your client about the merits of the position being taken. Alternatively, you may be responsible for helping to put the client's irrational fears to bed. Perhaps even more daunting, you may have to help some clients understand why the enormous amount of time spent on their case is fair and reasonable.

The selling continues once you make partner at the top law firm. At that point, you need to refine your sales pitch; and hopefully, you have a well-developed niche within your practice area to target new prospects. The law firm has a marketing department with helpful, nice people, but they are there for support. You generate the ideas and the business plan and get to work. The marketing people can help you get out your brand with beautiful brochures, but your ideas and action steps ultimately determine whether you succeed.

Effective sales pitches are also required if you decide to leave the law firm for a prestigious government job or perhaps a job in-house at a major corporation. If you are close to the time when you are supposed to make partner, you could be asked why you have not made partner; or whether you will be considered; and if not, why not. You could also be asked why you would want to leave the high salary. An effective sales pitch along with some strong recommendations from important people at the firm will be helpful here. Of course, to obtain the recommendations, you will need to have been effective at selling your strengths to the firm partners.

If you are not comfortable as a salesman, plenty of quality legal jobs are available, but perhaps a top law firm (AmLaw 100 or other) is not the best place for you. You may want to consider a career in the government or as in-house counsel, so that you do not have to constantly sell yourself, at least in the areas of obtaining clients and generating work projects. Even outside the law firm environment, in the area of obtaining work assignments, some selling can be involved in the competition among peers for interesting projects.

If you can handle the prospect of selling, and you have followed (to the extent possible) the GPS (as discussed in Chapter 1), it is time to market yourself to top law firms. Chapter 3 outlines the principles for getting into a top law firm.

CHAPTER 3
How to Get Into a Top Law Firm

TAP 3: To get into a top law firm, take a DIP:

1. Distinguish yourself.
2. Interview with people who care.
3. Practice persistence.

This chapter provides a systematic approach for getting into a top law firm whether or not you hail from a top-20 law school or you have excellent grades. The advice is organized into three straightforward principles. Each principle contains detailed guidance in the form of action steps to assist with implementation. The information is generally based on common threads in the stories of many successful candidates who get into top firms. The usefulness of this approach is confirmed at the end of this chapter by comments from hiring partners and associates at top firms concerning the value of one or more of the three principles.

The three common threads in the stories of successful candidates who get into top firms is that they generally (1) distinguish themselves from others in some meaningful way that demonstrates seriousness of purpose or commitment to a particular practice area (i.e., previous work experience, academic background, special skills such as bilingual, moot court champion, etc.); (2) target and seek informational interviews with lawyers that they believe (with good reason and after thoughtful research) are interested enough in their experience or background to grant them the meeting; and (3) practice persistence throughout the process to help make it happen. Put more succinctly, the successful job candidates take a DIP and get into a top firm by Distinguishing themselves, Interviewing with people who care, and Practicing persistence.

The rest of this chapter presents detailed information about each of the three principles and the underlying action steps involved in taking a DIP.

PRINCIPLE 1: DISTINGUISH YOURSELF

As discussed in Chapter 1, there is no formal declaring of a major in law school. However, you can distinguish yourself by demonstrating a strong interest in and commitment to a particular area and a sub-specialty within that area of the law. This idea was covered in Chapter 1, steps 2 and 3: pick a major and specialize. It is addressed again here because these are the most important steps you can take to secure a top law firm position.

The sections that follow provide some additional advice concerning how to go about distinguishing yourself (i.e., picking a major and specializing). They also reemphasize some of the networking techniques discussed in Chapter 1. To distinguish yourself: (1) follow the high marks; (2) look to previous experience; (3) start with a familiar subject; (4) seek answers from alumni; (5) do not overlook professors; (6) gain practical experience; and (7) consider engaging in the activities.

Follow the High Marks

A reasonable choice would be an area of law in which you have a strong academic record (even if that record consists of just a couple of law school courses). If you are interested in tax law, for example, your grades in tax courses may be a more reliable indicator of how you will perform at the firm than your grade in constitutional law or some other first-year course. Some people may disagree with you, but at least put yourself in a stronger position by being able to make your case on this basis.

Look to Previous Experience

Another reasonable choice would be an area in which you have previous work experience either directly or indirectly related to the practice area. Maximize this experience by arming yourself with written recommendation letters that confirm your proficiency in a specific area of law based on your performance in these positions.[1]

---

1. The significance of previous work experience was highlighted at a June 2011 roundtable, where one participant stated that "employers are recruiting for particular positions as opposed to the best available athlete. Or at least expecting the candidates to be able to articulate, in a very focused way, a particular practice area or practice areas in which they are interested." NALP June 2011 Roundtable.

Start With a Familiar Subject

A bit of a chicken-and-egg problem might be involved here. You may not know exactly where you should work during your law school summers, because you have not decided on which type of law you want to practice.[2]

In this case, start with a subject matter that is somewhat familiar to you, if possible. An obvious one is a subject related to your undergraduate major. Picking something familiar may increase your chances that what you pick will stick. Then you can tell a prospective employer that you had the plan of practicing that type of law all along.

Seek Answers from Alumni

If you are not sure what area you want to focus on, make a point to connect with 10 or more alumni from your law school with whom you share two or more characteristics. (These are referred to as touchpoints, in Chapter 1 and discussed again in the context of securing interviews after distinguishing yourself in principle 2 in this chapter.) Ask these alumni about their career path and what it is like to practice in their area of law.

Touchpoints are topics that enable you to relate to another person's life. They may be traits, and they may be experiences you have in common. Examples include personal relationships (spouses, children, siblings), past experiences (same high school, undergraduate school, law school, work experience), common interests (sports fan, playing sports previously or currently, similar hobbies), and similar backgrounds (religion, culture, same hometown or region of country or foreign country). Obtain lists of alumni with whom you might have some touchpoints from the career services center at your law school. Ask the people at the center to prepare different lists, perhaps starting with alumni with whom you have the most in common and narrowing the touchpoints from there.

Note that the law of averages applies here: if you want to double your success rate, you likely will have to double the requests you make. As

---

2. These days, law schools seem to be making more of an effort to get this information to students. For instance, Harvard Law School launched a problem-solving class for first-year students, and Stanford Law School is considering offering a full-time clinical course that involves several 40-hour-plus weeks of actual case work. Patrick Lee, *Law Schools Get Practical*, WALL STREET JOURNAL, July 11, 2011. As another example, the George Washington University Law School provides career panels covering various legal disciplines. The school also hosts a Career Exploration Conference, an event set up like a job fair and featuring lawyers in different practice areas who talk with students about their area of practice. Georgetown University has a similar program. Law students are well advised to attend as many of these programs as possible.

a frame of reference, telemarketers generally have a success rate of one in 10. That is, for every 10 cold calls, they may secure one appointment for an in-person meeting. Hopefully, alumni (especially those who volunteered to be part of the school's network) will be more receptive to you than strangers are to telemarketers. If not, it may help to have these numbers in mind.

When making your request, ask each person if it is possible to meet somewhere convenient for them (presumably by or at their office) for a couple of minutes for morning coffee, nothing more. Your goal for each of these meetings is not to obtain a job (and your communications should make that clear). Instead, your mission is twofold: to learn as much as possible about the actual practice of different areas of law, and to obtain one or two names and the contact information for people whom the person you are meeting with thinks would be helpful to you.

Do Not Overlook Professors

Develop a personal relationship with as many professors as possible. Let them know your interest in working in the area they teach or at least in learning more about what a lawyer actually does in that area of law. You never know how they can help or who they know.

Gain Practical Experience

Once you have a practice area in mind, you can demonstrate your interest by obtaining temporary employment in that area, and perhaps one unintended result of your informational networking could be a job opportunity. The employment could be a part-time job during law school or a stint during your summers after your first or second year.

One idea is to look for an opportunity where you can "work" as a law clerk at a firm that specializes in the area in which you are interested. Such positions at least offer the potential to learn some substantive skills, such as writing and thinking like a lawyer (in addition to doing so-called grunt work such as document review). This opportunity may present itself in the form of a nontraditional job for someone in law school such as a paralegal or even working for free in the right situation. There are no guarantees that this role will turn into something more, but why not put yourself in an environment where some heavy lifting is possible as well as potentially multiple opportunities to interact with firm lawyers?

Consider Other Activities

You can demonstrate commitment to a specialty in other ways. For example, take the patent bar if you are interested in intellectual property law, or sit for the Certified Public Accounting exam if you are interested in tax law. If litigation interests you, consider participating in moot court or similar competitions. Other options include serving as a research assistant for a particular professor, participating in a legal clinic, or working/interning in the public sector on a current issue in your area (i.e., for a member of Congress or a congressional committee working on major legislation in your chosen field).

Once you have selected your area of focus and shown some commitment to the subject, you will be in a better position. You can now demonstrate to a potential employer that the risk involved in hiring you is diminished, relative to hiring other candidates who do not possess similar academic focus and record, or experience, or both in the particular field. Moreover, picking a specialty is an important precursor to principle 2, interviewing with people who care. Making a choice will help you concentrate your search on firms and lawyers with capabilities in that area and thus provide you another touchpoint for networking purposes.

PRINCIPLE 2: INTERVIEW WITH PEOPLE WHO CARE

After distinguishing yourself, interview with as many lawyers as possible who may be interested in whatever it is that distinguishes you. To connect with these lawyers, try these five action steps: (1) research touchpoints; (2) write a letter, as in the old days; (3) follow up after sending the letter; (4) treat the "informational" meeting like an interview; and (5) follow up after the meeting.

Many of these steps will require the practice of persistence, principle 3, discussed in more detail following this discussion.

Research Touchpoints

You first researched touchpoints to connect with people who could provide information about different legal fields for purposes of picking a specialty and distinguishing yourself. This time you will have an additional touchpoint, which is an interest in your chosen field of law, and the purpose of meeting people is to discuss opportunities in the field now that you have proven yourself worthy by distinguishing yourself.

As with picking a specialty, for purposes of securing information interviews, find as many touchpoints as you can. But this time, look for touchpoints with about 50 to 100 people in the city or cities where you would like to practice. Again, once you have decided on a specialty, the career services office at your law school can provide you with valuable informational resources, including an alumni network database, to help you identify lawyers working in the area where you have chosen to focus. In addition, the career counselors can help you narrow down your list further to alumni with a specific number of your touchpoints. Presumably, they will connect you with people who have volunteered their contact information and so are likely to be receptive to your meeting request. When gathering your list, look for partners or senior associates so that you can meet with potential decision makers to *softly* make your case for how you could contribute to a top firm. Softly is stressed here, because you do not want to come on too strong. You want to demonstrate that you are mindful that the meeting you secure will likely be an "informational" interview. For more guidance on this point, see the tips below in Step 5 titled "Treat the Informational Meeting Like an Interview."

In addition to working with the career counselors, ask the professors who teach in the niche area you are targeting for contact information about alumni or others they know whom you could contact to discuss opportunities in this field.

Outside the career services office, you can perform your own search using social media sites such as LinkedIn, Twitter, and Facebook. Using LinkedIn, for example, you can search specific firms that specialize in the practice area for which you have chosen to focus and determine whether people who have a current or former relationship with that firm are connected to other people you know. If so, you can ask your personal contact to connect you. For guidance on maximizing the use of LinkedIn, see Dennis Kennedy and Allison C. Shields, *LinkedIn in One Hour for Lawyers* (Law Practice Management Section, American Bar Association, March 2012).

In addition, Twitter is a valuable networking tool. This site allows you to connect with people you do not know, based on common interests. One of those common interests could be a specific area of the law. Through Twitter you can reach out to these people (tweet) to discuss opportunities they may know about in the field. Also, Twitter has a program called Twellow, which allows you to search biographies and URLs. Using this program, you should be able to perform a search on specific law firms, identify lawyers associated with that firm, and reach out to those people.

Facebook also can be a useful resource, particularly for connecting with current friends or acquaintances and reconnecting with people from your past. Any of them might have some association (or know someone with an association) to law firms for which you are interested.

Traditional sites such as Martindale-Hubble, LexisNexis, or even Google might also help you in developing the lawyer pool you intend to target. For these sites, start your searches with the same undergraduate or graduate schools (preferably both), and combine them with the niche area in which you have some experience and interest.

Write a Letter

After performing your due diligence, write letters to the lawyers you locate in your search rather than sending an e-mail. Preparing a letter may indicate that you are the type of person who puts thought into how you present yourself and that you are someone who does not take shortcuts. The letter should be brief, but detail your experience. It should also explain that you are writing to that person because you went to the same schools (or whatever the relevant touchpoint is) and you understand that he or she practices in an area of law in which you are focusing.

In your letter, explain that you are writing to request a short meeting (one cup of coffee, not lunch) to brainstorm about opportunities in that particular practice area. It is important for the recipients to understand that you are not meeting to discuss opportunities at their firm. Most people will not want to meet with you if the purpose is to talk about jobs at that firm, especially given how difficult they are to come by without going through the firm's summer program. However, by explaining that the purpose is to talk about jobs in general and about the person's experience and career highlights in particular, you have a better chance of securing the meeting.

One idea that can help you get the meeting is to send the lawyer a relevant article that you wrote, or a recent one that you saw. Mention that he or she might be interested in the article, based on the firm's client base or scope of practice. This step would kill two birds with one stone by demonstrating that you did your research and that you are someone who could be worth meeting.

Follow Up After Sending the Letter

Do not be discouraged if you do not receive a response from the lawyer. He or she may be busy and travel frequently or simply may not want to respond. You likely will not receive a response to your request, which is okay because that was not the real purpose of sending the letter. The purpose was to introduce yourself, to demonstrate your interest and sincerity, and to have something to refer to in later calls.

After about 10 days or so, call the firm's main line and ask for the name of the assistant who works with the lawyer you wrote. Then direct-dial the company's information number and ask to be transferred to the assistant. Do not call expecting to talk to the lawyer, and do not ask for the lawyer unless you are prepared to go to voicemail and experience another non-response. When you are transferred to the assistant, be very friendly and explain that you are following up on a letter you sent requesting a short face-to-face meeting with the lawyer. Explain that you wrote because that lawyer is doing what you want to do, and you went to the same schools. You might even say that you were referred to the lawyer (which could technically be true if the career services office provided his name and contact information). After saying that you understand what busy schedules lawyers have, ask whether the assistant can recommend a good time to connect with the lawyer; or if it would be possible and appropriate for him or her to put you directly on the lawyer's schedule in the morning or some other time for a couple of minutes. What does the assistant recommend? Before you hang up, ask politely whether it would be okay if you followed up in a couple of days, assuming the advice is to leave a message.

When making the first couple of "sales" calls, you might find it difficult not to sound too aggressive (and some firms may not give you the time of day). But, with practice, you should be able to charm one or two assistants and tell him or her how much it would mean to you to have a couple minutes with the lawyer. If you are not successful in securing the meeting (or moving the process along closer to setting up a meeting date), try again in a couple of days. Obviously, do not harass the assistant; but try to follow up at least two times by phone after sending the letter. Make a chart to document your progress. If you are making no progress, move to the next name; but make sure you have given it some real effort. Repeat this process for all of the names on your list, and you should be able to secure a couple of informational interviews.

Treat the Informational Meeting Like an Interview

Once you secure some face-to-face meetings, which you are almost certain to do after making three contacts for 50 to 100 different people, treat these meetings as if you were going to an interview. Dress professionally, come early, and bring your resume and writing sample. More specifically, the sections below address various items to consider for your meeting, including: (1) mind-set; (2) tone; (3) what to say; (4) questions to ask about the lawyer; (5) questions to ask about the firm; (6) two goals; and (7) follow-up. These same items should be considered for formal interviews as well, especially the four must-ask questions about the firm discussed below.

Mind-Set

Be concise and make yourself as attractive as possible. Act as if you are on a job interview and your mission is to make the case for why you should be hired at that firm. However, keep in mind that the person you are meeting has agreed to an informational interview only, likely with the understanding that the purpose was to talk about opportunities outside of that firm. Accordingly, treat it in your mind as a real interview, but be sure to couch your comments in terms of what you believe you can contribute to similar firms that are hiring using, by way of example, the characteristics of this firm and the lawyer with whom you are meeting.

Tone

Be as modest as possible, especially since this person is doing you a favor by granting you the meeting. Use soft words such as "I believe" versus "I know" or "I will."

Also, consider finding a healthy balance between having limited emotion and being too excitable. Energetic and enthusiastic is great to an extent if that is who you are, but you may want to tone it down a bit so that you appear calm and relaxed, especially in a law firm setting. This approach may provide you some flexibility in that you likely will be able to connect with the quiet, intellectual type as well as the outgoing, gregarious type who usually does not want to be overshadowed, especially by you.

What to Say

Your so-called elevator speech should provide specifics about how you can contribute right away to any firm's practice. At the meeting, talk about your commitment to (background, experience, etc.) and laser-like focus on the specific area of law. Without saying it directly, your pitch should demonstrate that you are a fit with this particular firm (or, again, firms with similar cultures to the one at this firm).

The most important point to communicate to a potential employer is specifically how you can make meaningful contributions immediately. Sure, you will need some substantive training and some time to learn the preferences and quirks of the partners you work with (and you want to convey this thought to establish that you can work well with all personality types). However, state that you should be considered (at another firm) because your relevant experience and background will enable you to hit the ground running. Provide specifics about why this is the case, but be succinct. Match your skills with what you think would be required of you based on your rigorous research of the firm's clients and the previous and current projects of the lawyer you are meeting with. For example, say, "I understand your firm represents several large clients in the area of xyz. I *think* (again, use this soft approach because you may be wrong) my current experience (as well as my studies in law school) in this area including xxx (some technical legal sub-specialty) could be of value to some of these clients."

For your research, the firm website and printed marketing materials are two sources of useful information about firm clients (type, size, industry, and perhaps client names) and types of projects. Contact the firm's marketing department and request firm brochures and other materials about the firm and its clients. You may also ask for help navigating around the website to access the information you need.

To learn about prior cases the firm handled, researching docket databases may be helpful because most cases do not go to trial (and even those that do reach trial are not reported). For more information about docket research and the mechanics of using the Internet for locating this information, see Carole A. Levitt, J.D., M.L.S., and Mark E. Rosch, *The Cybersleuth's Guide to the Internet: Conducting Effective Investigative & Legal Research on the Web* (12th ed., 2012, IFL Press).

To demonstrate your compatibility with the firm culture, try to match your tone to that of the lawyer's tone and style (as discussed earlier). Specifically, consider your volume and energy level and make sure there is not an obvious disparity (up or down) between you and the lawyer.

Other than your elevator speech, additional talking points are good to have as preparation but it is probably best not to feel the need to cover all of them. You want to come across as comfortable (looking for the right opportunity to contribute versus a job) and relaxed with your message so it is not the end of the world if you do not get through your list.

Questions to Ask about the Lawyer

On your talking points list, make sure to include a couple of thoughtful questions about the lawyer you are meeting. Study his or her background, including the projects he or she is working on currently or has worked on in the past. You want to be in a position to ask the person a substantive question about his or her work. This preparation shows you have done your homework and allows the person to talk about themself, usually one's favorite subject.

Questions to Ask about the Firm

Firm Protocol

Here are some more specific questions, whose answers will help you compare opportunities across different firms (again, with the mind-set that this is a real interview even though it is informational and even though you are couching your questions and responses in terms of opportunities at other firms). In the worst-case scenario, the interview will not lead to getting a job at this lawyer's firm, but at least you will have refined your interviewing skills for the next interview.

What is the process of assigning work projects?

Are you responsible for keeping your plate full, or does someone else at the firm have that responsibility?

What happens if there are periods of time with little or no projects? Is there a working system in place for dividing projects (to prevent this result)?

Is face time around the office important, or is telecommuting acceptable sometimes if the work gets done?

How is each lawyer's performance measured? Are there additional metrics that matter other than the statistical information such as billable hours and collections?

How much face time will you have with clients as a junior associate, a mid-level associate, and a senior associate?

Do you have an "up or out" policy or alternative career paths? In other words, if you do not want to sell work (or choose not to), can you still be successful here in the long term as a service partner?

What type of training can you expect to receive at the firm both in terms of substantive skills (e.g., how to write a contract) and so-called soft skills (such as how to run a successful conference call with the client or other law-yers or both)? On a related note, does the firm reimburse continuing educa-tion through Practicing Law Institute (PLI) programs or other methods?

How often are employees reviewed? By whom? According to what cri-teria?

What is the firm's (and perhaps even more important, the practice group's) turnover statistics over the past two years, five years, and 10 years? Get the stats for associates and partners.

Is the firm (and practice group) growing? What is the firm's growth tar-get? What steps is the firm taking to reach this target?

How is the firm managed? Where is the firm managed from?

Does the firm have a strategic plan? If so, who contributes to the plan? Are there sufficient resources in place to support the plan?

Is the firm in sync with recent trends in the market? If not, this fact is not necessarily a negative. Some firms have high-highs and low-lows. That is great when the market is booming. Some may have low-highs (firm does not do as well as others in good times) and high-lows (firm does well in down economy, which may look attractive to you at this time).

Four Must-Ask Questions
At each informational meeting, you may want to ask the partners and asso-ciates you meet with how to provide information about the following four items: (1) people at the firm, (2) quality of work (both clientele and oppor-tunity to do heavy lifting), (3) opportunity for growth and development; and (4) compensation. Keep in mind that these questions may also be a bit premature if the meeting is really informational. However, it is important to keep these items in the back of your mind whenever interviewing, so that you can assess whether it is worth your time and energy to pursue the potential opportunity. Although people may have different preferences and priorities when picking a top firm, a reasonable approach would be to select a firm that offers pleasant people, interesting work, plenty of opportunity for professional growth and development, and a reasonable salary.

The People
This firm attribute may be the most important factor, even above the quality of the work. If you have stimulating work but find your col-leagues difficult, you may be unhappy. On the other hand, if your work is not perfect but you enjoy the people, odds are that you would not be

miserable. Could you see yourself comfortably spending long days (and sometimes long nights) with the people you meet? It is difficult to know for sure when everyone is on his or her best behavior in an interview setting. One item that may help make your decision is whether any of the lawyers you meet go out of their way for you during the courting process. For example, is there someone who is extra helpful about providing information on firm timing and next steps (and regularly available to answer additional lingering questions about the firm) such that you feel a sincere interest on their part? If so, that lawyer may be a good candidate to be your sponsor (have your back, so to speak), which will be helpful to you as you advance. Chapter 4 details how to succeed once you are employed at a top law firm.

The Quality and Type of Work
Will you have the opportunity to do heavy lifting? How soon? Would you have the best opportunity to focus on the area of work you think you may enjoy? Will you be able to receive quality training?

Professional Development Opportunities
Does the firm suggest that growth and development are a priority? Will you be able to take on increasing responsibility in terms of type of work, interface with clients, mentoring younger lawyers, leadership roles at the firm, and so on? Are you encouraged to speak and write? Is there a clear transition plan so that older partners could train younger partners to eventually take a lead role in the firm's client matters? What is the track to partner? Are there multiple tracks (i.e., income and equity partners)?

Compensation
Note that compensation is at the end of the list because generally top firms are fairly comparable in this regard, especially in the beginning, but obviously it is important, especially as you become more senior. What is the starting salary? Lockstep or merit-based increases? Bonus ranges?

Two Goals for the Interview
Your two goals for the interview are: (1) to set up the potential for fugure contact with that person; and (2) to obtain contact information of other people. Find a reason to have another contact with that person. At the end of the meeting, you want to have a purpose for continuing the contact in

addition to sending the normal follow-up (thank you for meeting me) letter. For example, perhaps you share a common interest such as sailing, golf, or college sports. Mentioning this interest provides another touchpoint and may help you to stand out or, at minimum, make you more likely to receive a response to your future communication. In addition, see if you can secure the contact information of one or two other people that person thinks would be helpful for you in your search. Armed with this information, you will be able to call those people and explain that the first person thought it might be a good idea to connect.

Follow-Up

Prepare a typewritten, sincere thank-you letter (handwritten may work if you have excellent penmanship). In the letter, address specific points about your conversation, particularly items that the lawyer you met with said and your thoughts about them. Send the letter in the next day's mail.

For the future, think of reasons to keep in contact with this person for your round two follow-up so you can stay on his or her radar screen. But the reasons have to be legitimate and not just fluff. Some examples of occasions for additional contact: (1) you win moot court; (2) you finish a writing sample; (3) something significant happens to you at your job; (4) someone wrote you a recommendation letter that attests to your brilliance, strong work ethic, or good character; (5) you earn some more excellent grades to report; and (6) you find an article that is relevant to the interviewer's practice. Note that it is okay to also include something personal such as something related to a sports team you both follow, but the main reason for following up should be substantive. Contact the lawyer again with the news in about three weeks or a month, sooner or later depending on whether you have something reasonable to say.

PRINCIPLE 3: PRACTICE PERSISTENCE

Lack of persistence is one of the major causes of failure. Moreover, experience with thousands of people has proved that lack of persistence is a weakness common to the majority of men. It is a weakness, which may be overcome by effort. The ease with which lack of persistence may be conquered will depend entirely upon the intensity of one's desire.

—Napoleon Hill, *Think and Grow Rich*

When I thought I couldn't go on, I forced myself to keep going. My success is based on persistence, not luck.

—Estee Lauder, entrepreneur

Good luck is another name for tenacity of purpose.

—Ralph Waldo Emerson

It is probably apparent that success with principle 2 (interview with people who care) will likely depend on your level of persistence. Persistence in this context means that generally you operate in a similar manner as a salesperson (preferably more genuine than certain used-car salesmen but just as tenacious) and that you are rigorous in your follow-up with each person you meet. Some people are turned off by this trait, but your goal is not to please everyone.

Persistent follow-up is a crucial step to secure the informational or other interview, but it is often not done at all—or not done well. Give the person you are following up with an "appropriate" amount of time to respond, but do not wait too long. The appropriate time is really based on facts and circumstances, including previous interactions and your good judgment.

Assuming you have provided the person some opportunity to respond, do not be afraid of turning them off. Some may think you are too aggressive, but that may be worth the risk if the alternative is waiting and wondering for eternity. Even if some people dislike your aggressiveness, others will be impressed. Remember that you have to get in, and your task may be more difficult if you do not hail from a top-20 law school or possess a high grade point average in all courses, not just your focus area. Many law students do not practice persistence, so it seems a good way to distinguish yourself from the herd fairly easily.

Part of persistence is having a thick skin and being comfortable with rejection. As you will learn, it may take a couple rounds of rejections before you are granted an interview, but if you want a top firm job, you may have to keep trying. If at some point you receive a formal rejection letter or oral, consider asking for feedback about it. In the worst-case scenario, the firm may decline to share the information with you. In the best-case scenario, they can provide constructive criticism on tangible things you may be able to correct for the future.

You may be wondering when it is reasonable to give up with respect to each particular firm. The answer is that it depends on the facts and circumstances of each case and your judgment about when enough is enough.

There certainly is an appropriate balance to strike between persistence and allowing things to happen naturally (or in the case of seeking interviews, moving on to the next firm). It is sometimes difficult to know when to stop pressing for fear of going overboard or because it won't help and wait for things to happen in due course or accept that they are not meant to happen for you at that time. Achieving the appropriate balance in this context may come over time after several experiences and greater reliance on your intuition.

COMMENTS FROM TOP FIRM HIRING PARTNERS

The significance of the three principles discussed in this chapter for taking a DIP and getting into a top law firm is confirmed by the following comments of hiring partners and associates at top firms.

Distinguish Yourself

- "Relevant prior work experience will often make a big difference. Firms benefit from associates who know the industry of a client and have work experience that relates to what the clients of the firm do."
- "Students should think hard about what they really want to do in their law careers, and try to focus on areas of practice they think will be interesting to them. While firms cannot always accommodate a specific practice interest, students who have a focus and are able to articulate why they are interested in an area will have an advantage."
- "Be able to articulate how your skills will benefit the firm—what about your background and experience will make you a good fit with the firm's culture and legal work?"

Interview with People Who Care

- "Referrals from firm clients, contacts of partners, or partners or associates who work at the firm count for a lot in the hiring process. So networking can really benefit you."

COMMENTS FROM TOP FIRM ASSOCIATES

Distinguish Yourself

- "One adjunct professor gave me the opportunity to extern at his firm, a top firm, during the spring semester. This was helpful from the point of view of enabling me to better understand what is expected of an attorney at a top firm and how to succeed in that environment."

- "I think my experience with DOJ—having handled my own case load and tried cases for the government for four years, including bankruptcy cases in Florida—was most beneficial. In interviewing for my position as a bankruptcy associate, I was able to offer my new firm someone who could immediately step in on a case, go to court, try cases, take depositions, conduct discovery, write briefs, and argue motions, without much additional training. While I did have a lot to learn substantively about bankruptcy law, my litigation skills enabled me to offer a valuable skill to my firm as a fourth-year lateral associate."

- "I came to realize the nature of work I was given is different from what I expected for my career. I was working on projects covering a variety of tax issues without the opportunity to specialize in international tax, the area I would like to focus on in my career. Therefore, I decided to pursue a position at a top firm and my first step was to become a part-time LL.M. student."

- "I excelled in all my courses in the area I wanted to practice, without exception. My friend has a more impressive story about distinguishing himself in that he joined the circus and worked his way up from clown extra to chief legal officer, and then got noticed by the hiring partner of a top firm that also happened to be an entertainment attorney. That's life under the bigtop for you!"

- "I worked for a solo practitioner my second summer. He was lead counsel on a significant litigation matter, and his co-counsel was a top firm. Over a period of several months I developed a great relationship with co-counsel (and worked with many of the firm's partners). I worked hard and showed people I was serious about being a litigator, which led to a job offer in the fall. I think others can have similar success if they put in a lot of effort at whatever legal job they can obtain during law school. Once you have made a good impression, you will be able to leverage your supervisor's relationships to open doors to top firms. Chances are your supervisor, whether at a legal aid clinic, a government agency, or a small firm, will have close friends that work at top firms. And a recommended candidate will always have a leg up on the competition."

Interview with People Who Care

- "Networking played a very important role in my job search. My entire strategy was based on making connections with attorneys with whom I had something in common."

- "I began in the middle of the fall semester by researching the names of attorneys at top firms who had attended Irish law schools. This was a laborious process; it involved going to the website of roughly 12 Irish-trained attorneys, both partners and associates. The next step I took was to contact each attorney by email over winter break asking for an informational interview. I attached my resume to each email. Some did not respond, some offered to speak with me by phone, and some invited me to meet them at their firm. I spent a few days of winter break in New York meeting the various attorneys, four associates and one partner. It was useful to meet with the associates from the point of view of learning about their job search experiences, but they were obviously not in a position to offer me a job. I met the partner at his firm for a 30-minute informational interview. Following this meeting, the firm contacted me and invited me back for a formal callback interview. I attended the interview the final week of January and received an offer the following week."

- "An important step was approaching my professors to express my job search concerns and ask for advice. My contacts and interviews with the two top firms came through recommendations by my professors. I was an evening student. I believe it was during the fall interview process (in the beginning of 3L for us evening students) that I realized that I had two great resources in the professors I was close to, and that I could not rely on the law school or the fall recruitment process."

- "The most important step for me is networking. Talking with professors, former partners and people they introduced me to helped me to build up my confidence, which was extremely important in the interview process. Networking gave me the opportunity to talk with many people who gave me valuable career advice. A few of them offered to pass my resume and introduced me to people who have insights on the jobs I am interested in."

- "Networking was helpful. While I secured the call for the interview on my own, after being invited to interview, I called a family friend who worked for the firm in another state, and asked him to put in a good word for me. When I had not received any communication after my interview, I again contacted that friend and asked him to follow up. He was very helpful in moving along the offer process. While I believe I "got my foot in the door" on my own, he was helpful in facilitating the process after that, although ultimately I got the offer on my own merits."

- "I think the most important thing is to identify a category of attorneys with whom you have something in common, e.g., same university or law school, and target your job search efforts. In my opinion, doing so increases the chances that the attorney contacted will read your email and resume and be willing to take some action on your behalf."
- "The most important step is to forge relationships with people you enjoy and who enjoy you."
- "The most practical of all advice is to leverage your connections. People are generally willing to help others look for jobs, and very few people will get a job by simply sending in a resume to a recruiting attorney."

Practice Persistence

- "While the process took some time, I remained persistent in my efforts to obtain this job. The best advice I can give is to be persistent, and pick yourself up when you get knocked down. I could wallpaper my house with all of the rejection letters I received over the years, but eventually you will find the right firm for you."
- "Networking is very helpful, as is persistence and preparation."
- "I believe I was ultimately successful in obtaining the position in a non-traditional manner due to forward planning and perseverance. I think that starting the process early and spending time on targeted research gave me an advantage."

Now that you have taken a DIP to get into a top law firm, you need to distinguish yourself as a top performer. Chapter 4 discusses the principle soft skills required to succeed as an associate at a top law firm.

CHAPTER 4
How to Succeed as an Associate at a Top Law Firm

TAP 4: To become a top-performing associate, develop and use these soft skills:

1. Determine and satisfy partner preferences.
2. Be rigorous.
3. Manage workload effectively.
4. Seek specific feedback and take action.
5. Make others look good.
6. Document performance results annually.
7. Have a partner's mind-set.
8. Secure an effective sponsor.

So you took a DIP and got into a top law firm. Congratulations. Now how do you continue to prove your value? Obviously, as a preliminary matter, you have to demonstrate substantive proficiency in your particular practice area. And the American Bar Association has books to help you in this regard for various practice areas.[1] But what else does an associate need to be successful in a law firm setting? How do you deal effectively with the idiosyncrasies of markedly different partners and clients with different demands and expectations? The intangible extra traits required are referred to as soft skills, defined as "personal attributes that enable someone to interact

---

1. For example, for how-to advice on performing the actual tasks of a commercial litigator, see Cristen Sikes Rose, THE COMMERCIAL LITIGATOR'S JOB: A SURVIVAL GUIDE (Chicago, American Bar Association, 2005).

effectively and harmoniously with other people."[2]

This chapter discusses eight soft skills that have helped many associates at top firms succeed and continue in the running as strong candidates for eventual admission as partners. Also included in this chapter is advice from current top-firm partners about these skills and other principles for success.

Admittedly, many of the concepts described in this chapter may be obvious and intuitive. However, that does not necessarily mean associates are practicing these principles. In fact, despite the increased competition for coveted spots at top law firms today, many associates do not follow most or even many of these principles. Accordingly, the informed and disciplined person may find it easy to stand out as a star performer.

The eight soft skills that follow are discussed in the order in which you are most likely to benefit from their use. For example, the first couple of skills, determine preferences and be rigorous, relate to advice for receiving, working on, and completing an assignment, all items you will deal with upfront and on a regular basis. Once you have that process working smoothly, you will benefit from having a partner's mind-set and securing an effective sponsor, both items that will be helpful as you become more senior.

This chapter describes each of the soft skills and how to apply them. It also discusses some adjustments that you may have to make to your soft skills when dealing with the different types of partners and clients.

SOFT SKILL 1: DETERMINE AND SATISFY PARTNER PREFERENCES

One of the keys to being a top performer at a top law firm is to determine the various preferences of the partners you work with and then to satisfy those preferences. Specifically, to work more effectively with the partner, (1) determine the various communication preferences surrounding an assignment, and satisfy those preferences; and (2) determine at least one defining skill of the partner (i.e., a silver tongue, a knack for analyzing and quickly getting to the bottom of complex legal issues, a strong writer, etc.) and emulate that skill, which he or she is likely to emphasize when you are working together. In the long run, the more familiar you become with the partner's communication preferences and unique talent upfront, the more time you will be able to focus on producing quality legal work.

To determine a partner's communication preferences, ask the partner be-

---

2. OED ONLINE (Oxford University Press, 2013), available at http://oxforddictionaries.com/us/definition/american_english/soft%2Bskills (last visited July 11, 2013).

fore a project is assigned about his or her general preferences. When a project is assigned, ask for preferences that are project specific. For general preferences and for insight as to the partner's unique talent, ask older associates who have worked with that partner. These associates will be able to answer some questions you may not have thought to ask. Also, the more of this information you can obtain from others, the more you can focus on substantive questions relating to the assignment when you meet with the partner.

Understand and Satisfy Communication Preferences

As a junior associate, you will have many opportunities to satisfy the communication preferences of the partners who should be treated like your clients in the early years. Several opportunities exist in the context of working on a project assigned by a partner. For example, each stage of the project—receiving the assignment, performing the work, and presenting the conclusions—gives the associate a chance to demonstrate understanding of partner preferences and satisfy those preferences.

Receiving the Assignment

When you receive a project from the partner, it will be helpful to understand (1) what is being asked of you substantively; (2) the format he or she would like you to use when responding to the issue (i.e., in a detailed memo, in an e-mail, in a short summary memo, all of the above, etc.); (3) approximately how much billable time the partner expects the project to require; and (4) the partner's timing and, if possible to determine, the end user's (firm client's) timing. Not surprisingly, many of these items are project specific.

What Question Are You Being Asked to Answer?

Understanding what is being asked of you is one of the most important steps. If your marching orders are unclear in any way, ask for clarification immediately or ask when you could return to confirm that you are on the same page—even if the partner is moving fast and seems to have little time. Few situations are worse than not being clear on the task assigned. You may be able to save yourself hours of time by taking a couple of extra minutes to ask questions on the front end.

To confirm your understanding, it may be helpful for you to restate, as precisely as possible, the partner's request. The partner is rarely interested only in what the applicable law is in the relevant jurisdiction; he or she also wants to know how to apply the law given the client's fact pattern or under various fact patterns, if you do not know some or all of your client's facts. So, for example, "I understand you want me to research the legal question under federal *X* law of *XYZ*, and provide information as to what facts are determinative to the result under present law without necessarily providing an answer/making a legal conclusion." Or, "I understand you want me to provide an answer and summarize the knowable facts that help me formulate my opinion."

There is one caveat to this advice about asking a lot of questions or confirming your understanding: You may want to determine from other associates who have worked with the partner whether the partner appreciates, or more to the point, tolerates many questions. Perhaps the partner is more of a big-picture type and prefers to leave the minutiae to someone else (you). If that is the case, it probably makes sense to save your questions for an associate or a friendly partner who has worked with the partner before and may be able to help confirm that you are on the right track.

Follow the Desired Format

Preferences vary widely from partner to partner. Make sure you understand how the partner wants the results of your work communicated, and follow that approach. Otherwise, you take a risk that even a high-quality legal product both in terms of writing style and substantive legal analysis will not be well received.

If the partner requests a formal memorandum, ask an associate who has worked with the partner to send you an example of a prior memorandum that was consistent with the partner's preferences. Consider also asking the partner for a sample document as well. It could not hurt to have two examples.

Similarly, if the partner wants only a one-pager or an e-mail message, ask for samples of those documents as well. In those cases, you may still want to prepare a regular memorandum for the file. However, be sensitive to the partner's timing, and make sure you provide the answer in the format specified when requested and worry about the niceties on your time.

Be Conscious of Time

With regard to time spent, some partners will tell you to bill everything and they will handle the write-offs if they think you have spent too much time on the matter. That advice to write everything down makes sense—but when you are starting out, you want partners to think of you as efficient so they are inclined to use you again in the future. Accordingly, if the partner tells you something should take 10 hours and you spend 20 hours, you may want to consider chalking up some of the extra time as learning and writing it down yourself before submitting your time entries—unless, of course, the issue being researched turned out to be the wrong question, a bit more difficult, or required some more steps than the partner envisioned. These scenarios happen frequently.

Over time you should be able to anticipate these potential hiccups and gauge timing more accurately.

Understand Timing and Manage Expectations

As far as timing, be sure you have some understanding of the partner's timing and whether you are given a real or merely an aspirational deadline. Perhaps the partner wants to hear from you five days before he or she meets with the client, just in case the project requires a second round and more or different digging which is generally the case. The more information you can obtain, the better, and this information will help you effectively manage expectations. Once you have the relevant information, assess your other responsibilities. Do not overpromise what you can do by which date including when you can provide preliminary information if desired. It may be helpful to communicate other time-sensitive projects on your plate to determine whether it makes sense to add this project to the list given the partner's timing. However, there is a delicate balance here because you probably do not want to turn down work as a junior associate.

Working on an Assignment

While working on a project from the partner, it will help you to understand the partner's communication preferences regarding interaction about the project, including method, time, and frequency of contact. The following questions all relate to general preferences and so, if possible, have them answered by an associate who has worked with the partner on several projects.

Method and Time of Contact

For example, does the partner prefer you stop by to ask a question, call, or send an e-mail message? It is important to follow some formalities when dealing with partners to respect their schedule. So popping in to discuss a project is generally not a good idea even if you have a friendly, informal relationship. Partners are busy, and they appreciate advance notice. They probably will not have time for you unless you schedule the meeting in advance.

On the topic of schedule, you should ask the following questions: What are the hours of the partners? Are they there early? Do they stay late? Are they usually around during the lunch hour? Do they have a particular time that they prefer to be alone (i.e., no visitors first thing in the morning)? Do they work at certain times on weekends (i.e., are they online Sunday night to get ready for the week)? Having this information will help you plan your schedule accordingly and help ensure you are meeting with partners when it is convenient for them.

Frequency of Contact

Understanding the partner's preference for frequency of contact also is helpful. For example, how often does the partner prefer you follow up regarding your status on a project? Every day? Every week? Does it depend on the type of project?

It is generally preferable to keep the communication ongoing, even when you do not have much to report. Partners tend to appreciate status reports about potential issues that have come up and estimated time for completion. For example, send an e-mail stating that "I wanted to let you know that I am still working on the matter, and I expect to have something for you tomorrow (or next week)." Sending this type of e-mail tends to be better than sending nothing and potentially making the partner wonder about the status—or worse, making the partner contact you first regarding status. To the greatest extent possible, it will be helpful if you can manage expectations on the project. In the beginning it may be difficult to assess how long something will take, especially if the matter covers an unfamiliar area. With time, though, you will get better at assessing your timing for future projects. Moreover, while the project is progressing and as you get further into it you can provide the partner with a more realistic idea of your timing.

Presenting Conclusions

When you have wrapped up the project, it will be helpful to understand the partner's communication preferences regarding presenting conclusions. These preferences may be project specific, so it may be best not to rely solely on information obtained ahead of time from an associate who has worked with the partner. Two issues that may come up are the partner's preferences for follow-up and for finalizing and transmitting your work product either internally or to the client.

Follow-up
For example, once you submit your assignment, how often can you check in to go over your work? Is every couple of days acceptable to the partner? Generally, it is never a good idea to hound a partner about whether he or she has had a chance to review the project. Even if some partners take a month or longer to review your work, that does not give you license to be aggressive. In that case, checking back every couple of weeks seems reasonable if done in a calm and relaxed manner, assuming you have confirmed that this approach is acceptable to the partner.

Finalizing and Transmitting Your Work Product
Finalizing and transmitting your work product triggers several questions. Their answers depend on who else is involved on the project and whether you are sending your work internally or to the client. First, assuming you have prepared a memorandum, ask who the partner wants listed in the "From" line as the author. You? The partner? Both you and the partner with the partner first? The name of the firm? This issue obviously takes on more significance if the memorandum is going to the client or even a partner in firm management.

Next, determine from the partner how he or she prefers to receive the work product from you. For example, the partner may prefer both a hard copy and an e-mail attachment, or just one or the other. If multiple firm attorneys are involved in the project, the partner may want you to send the work product to everyone by e-mail, or the partner may want you to hold off until he or she has reviewed your conclusions. In the case of multiple people, the partner may also want you to include a short summary of the main points of the memorandum in the e-mail, so others can know the gist in case they do not have a chance to review the document.

Sending e-mails to multiple people requires sensitivity. Make sure you have included everyone who was supposed to be included. Also make sure you have satisfied the partner's preference to the extent he or she has one, and many do regarding the ordering of the e-mail recipients and the parallel salutation if you include one in the e-mail message. One option is straight alphabetical order. Another option is to start by listing the most important partner on the engagement, generally the billing partner or relationship partner. A third option is to list the relationship partner first and list the remaining names in alphabetical order. If the e-mail is going to the client, the partner will likely have a preference about how many lawyers to include because he or she anticipates the client's potential complaint that too many lawyers are involved.

Titles are also important. Be sure that you understand the partner's preference for titles for himself, other partners, and the client in formal memoranda and e-mail communications. Partners in firm management may be particularly sensitive about titles. As with most of these issues, it cannot hurt to be too careful and confirm that your planned approach is consistent with the partner's preferences.

In addition to understanding and satisfying the various communication preferences of the partner, it is helpful to understand and commit to emulating a defining skill of the partner.

Understand and Emulate a Defining Skill of the Partner

Do the partners have a particular skill that distinguishes them and on which they place heavy emphasis? How best can you learn this skill from them? Identifying this partner strength up front should prove helpful in providing context for some of their future comments and requests. In particular, this knowledge may put into perspective certain feedback from partners that may appear to be overly harsh or critical. Instead of taking the comments personally, you will be in a position to recognize the teaching moment and continue working toward emulating that particular skill.

To illustrate different operating styles, consider the following three hypothetical partners with different strengths commonly found among top firm partners.[3] Also think about the learning opportunities each style presents.

One partner may be very articulate and command a room. You may be able to learn from her by observing, listening, and taking notes in various settings. For example, on a conference call, note how she waits until all others have spoken to make her point. Moreover, she is careful not to appear to undermine anyone and instead offers them praise ("because they are the experts") even though her ultimate opinions are quite different from those previously expressed.

Another partner may excel at analyzing difficult legal questions and formulating advice for the client. You may be able to learn from him by studying his process or asking him about particular methods used. For example,

---

3. Some top firm partners exhibit all three of the skills discussed, and some possess none of them. The examples are exaggerated to more easily demonstrate the potential learning opportunities.

note his thoughtfulness in tackling an issue to be resolved, first by spending some time attempting to narrow the precise legal question or questions to be answered.[4] That step may save him lots of time on the back end. Next, observe his thoroughness—even when he thinks he may have found the answer, he lives his mantra to "keep reading," which can be especially important when trying to understand the exceptions to the applicable law being researched.

Still another partner may be known for effective legal writing, so that laypeople like clients can understand the reasoning in his memoranda. You may be able to learn from him by studying his writing method or asking him for general tips on how to write effectively. For example, note his pattern of using repetition to make his writing easier to follow by stating concepts multiple times in different ways. Do not be fooled though; despite this use of repetition, every word used in the memorandum carries freight (i.e., if it is not needed, it is deleted).

---

4. This practice was discussed earlier as part of understanding and satisfying the partner's communication preferences.

ACCORDING TO CURRENT TOP LAW FIRM SENIOR PARTNERS:
Receiving Work Assignments

- "I always appreciate an associate approaching me for work, although I have no problem approaching him or her. Such pro-activity suggests great interest in the firm and a career here."
- "He should share information about other assignments if he thinks it's germane or if he needs help sorting out priorities."
- "When receiving an assignment, the associate should ask how much time I have to discuss the assignment right then, and tailor his/her inquiries accordingly."
- "If you don't understand what I'm asking for or need guidance, ask. Always ask when I need the answer by and in what form I need it."

Working on Projects

- "If there is a great deal of 'learning' time, I want to discuss how much should be written down. More experienced associates are more susceptible to compensation penalty for poor realization statistics."
- "I want to know the status of the assignment even if there is no news and the associate should check-in at least every couple of days."
- "The more experienced he or she is, the more I would prefer him/her to ask follow up questions in order to better actualize on his/her higher hourly rate."
- "Don't ask me for the answer. If I knew it, I wouldn't be asking you."
- "Tell me what you think. Don't be afraid to voice your opinion."
- "Don't fail to respond within a reasonable time to a call or an e-mail from me requiring a response during work hours."

ACCORDING TO CURRENT TOP LAW FIRM SENIOR PARTNERS:
Presenting Conclusions
- "As with most other things, before presenting his or her conclusions, he/she should simply ask me my preferred format. I usually like to discuss the answer before a lot of time is spent (and potentially wasted) commemorating it. This is my preference even with summer associates."
- "It is always a good idea for the associate to allow enough time before the deadline to revise after presenting the initial conclusions."

SOFT SKILL 2: BE RIGOROUS

Another one of the keys to being a top performer at a top law firm is to approach all tasks in a rigorous manner. It seems obvious that this soft skill should be practiced, but many associates do not appreciate the point that consistently being rigorous can distinguish you from peers when partners are assigning work or when partner time comes.

To help you execute this soft skill, consider the following advice about ways to be rigorous when performing legal research and writing. Associates at top law firms spend much of their time on these two activities.

Research

A successful research project is one in which you have demonstrated to the partner, in a reasonable period of time, (i) your laser-like focus in identifying the precise legal question to be answered, and (ii) articulating how experts in the area have analyzed this issue or one closely related by analogy, if no authority exists that is directly on point. You may be asked to apply the client's facts to the law, but you will most likely not have all or even any of the client's facts. Thus you will have to identify the moving parts, or lay out the particular facts that would tilt the scales one way or the other given the legal test. Due to deadlines and cost considerations, you will always have a balance to strike between being efficient and scorching the earth until you are sure you have gotten to the bottom of a legal issue.

To help you accomplish the goals just described, follow these two steps when performing research assignments: start with the background, and keep reading.

Start with the Background

One way to help demonstrate your research rigorousness is to start from the beginning and make sure you understand the purpose for the rules. To determine the purpose, analyze what rules were in place before the current law and determine why the policy makers in Congress believed the rules needed to change or why they created new law covering items not previously covered. Similarly, if the rules are regulatory as opposed to statutory, review the agency's thinking at the time the rules were promulgated. Additionally, review how the courts were analyzing the relevant legal issues around the time the rules were enacted. Lastly, study what legal experts in the area were saying around that time. Consulting legislative history, preambles underlying relevant regulations, and caselaw as well as relevant journals, periodicals, and press covering the particular legal area should prove helpful in answering these questions about background.

Keep Reading

Another way to demonstrate your research rigorousness is to keep reading, particularly in practices that are heavily rules based and technical. As one example, in the area of tax law, it is crucial to read an entire statute, line by line and page by page, in the Internal Revenue Code where the exceptions and the exceptions to the exceptions often swallow the general rule. The same goes for the underlying Treasury Regulations which sometimes contain helpful examples or language twenty or so pages deep. For secondary legal authorities, such as law review articles and treatises, it is helpful to keep reading until you find material that presents or at least raises the possibility of conflicting sides of a legal position, so that you can acknowledge to the partner that there is another argument and articulate your reasoning as to why you believe one side is more persuasive.

A related point is to make sure what you keep reading is the current law assuming that current law is the law that is applicable; in some cases, it may not be. This tip is especially important for areas of law that are frequently changing.

Writing

Two reasonable goals when writing for a partner are to articulate difficult concepts succinctly and in a user-friendly manner. In many cases, your reasoning may be more valuable to the partner than your ultimate conclusion. To help accomplish these goals, follow these steps when producing legal memoranda or other written work: (1) start with the baby case; (2) use repetition; (3) use your final draft as your starting point; (4) ask another's opinion; and (5) confirm that you are on the right track.

Start with the Baby Case

One way to help demonstrate your writing rigorousness is to assume the reader of your memorandum knows nothing. To help get the reader easily into the issue, begin the analysis section of the memorandum with an explanation of the so-called baby case, which is a basic fact pattern along with a description of the applicable, noncontroversial black-letter law that applies to that fact pattern. Next, provide a short summary of the general landscape surrounding your legal issue before getting into the particular issue at hand. For example, what do industry groups, other practitioners, or academics identify as the overall hot issue(s) in this area? Finally, distinguish the baby case from your case by describing what facts are different to the extent that you know the facts and by stating the legal questions and nuances raised by your case.

Use Repetition

Another way to demonstrate writing rigorousness is to use repetition. Make the writing easier to follow by stating concepts three times. First, summarize what you are going to say upfront. Then, provide the detail in the body. Lastly, conclude with another summary of what was just said.

Use Your Final Draft As Your First Draft

A third way to demonstrate writing rigorousness is to use as your starting draft the document you believe is your final draft and ready to hand over to the partner. Then, proofread, rewrite, and proofread again that version multiple times until the substance and style are perfect.

Regarding substance, proofread the draft to confirm that the cases and other sources listed actually support the proposition cited. In other words, you want to verify that the memorandum is technically accurate. A technically inaccurate memorandum is worthless even if well written. A related point is to make sure that you have sufficiently made your case. Ensure that you have thoroughly covered any exceptions to the rule and have adequately dealt with counterarguments, assuming you provide a conclusion.

Regarding style, make sure the point of the document is clear and provided up front. A layman should be able to follow your writing and understand the reason for the document. Obviously, poor style and grammatical mistakes will take away from a technically accurate, substantively strong memo.

Ask Another's Opinion

A fourth way to demonstrate writing rigorousness is to have another partner or senior associate read your memorandum before finalizing. That person could be particularly helpful for weighing in on whether the point of your memo is clear, makes sense, and is supported by the law cited. If you are asking an associate, offer to treat him or her to lunch. If you are asking a busy partner, offer to treat him or her to a very nice lunch.

Confirm that You Are on the Right Track

A fifth way to demonstrate writing rigorousness is to confirm with the partner who assigned the project that you are doing what he or she asked you to do both in terms of substance you are answering the right question and style (you are writing logically and coherently from that person's perspective). For example, for this project, is the partner looking for a conclusion or just the legal test that can be applied to any fact pattern? Should the conclusion be stated up front? Does the partner prefer two documents, one executive summary with the conclusion and a longer one supporting the conclusion?

Confirming you are on the partner's page with this particular project builds upon your initial step of determining the partner's general preferences before you started the project.[5] Now the question is whether your work reflects an accurate understanding of the preferences stated. Note, however, that you must definitely strike a balance here as to the type and amount of questions you ask at this point. You want to be thought of as someone who can get things done without hand-holding, but you also want to be rigorous (again, in how you approach an issue substantively and in how you communicate your findings stylistically) and consistent with partner preferences. Some partners are more willing than others to offer confirmation feedback, so just be sensitive to the particular partner's appetite for questions and adjust your method accordingly.

---

5. See soft skill 1 discussion about determining and satisfying partner communication preferences.

ACCORDING TO CURRENT TOP LAW FIRM SENIOR PARTNERS:
Writing
- "Always give me your best product. I expect to review, correct and comment on drafts. I don't expect to correct grammar and spelling nor do I expect to do your thinking for you."
- "The quality of the work product should reflect the opinion that the associate wants me to have of him/her. Deadlines can be malleable; quality work is not."
- "It comes down to convincing the senior lawyer that you and your work can be trusted. If I know that you will give me a polished piece of work when I expect it, I will keep knocking on your door to do more. If not, you cannot be a dependable member of my team and I have to worry that I won't be able to deliver what I have promised to the client or the court."
- "Don't ever expect me to take my time to edit your written work for grammar, syntax or punctuation."
- "Write clearly and concisely."

SOFT SKILL 3: MANAGE WORKLOAD EFFECTIVELY
A third key to being a top performer at a top law firm is to manage your workload effectively. From day one as a top law firm associate, you are marketing yourself to all of the partners in your group. The idea is to become invaluable to as many partners as possible both for job security and to maximize your opportunities to do interesting work. Accordingly, your continuing goals are to (1) keep a full plate of projects while being realistic about how much you can handle under time pressure; (2) communicate time commitments; and (3) follow through.

Keep a Full Plate
One component of managing work effectively as a law firm associate is to keep a continually full plate. Also ensure that plate is made up of primarily billable projects.

Billable Projects
There are at least three reasons it is important to be efficient enough to

handle multiple projects at once and continually keep a full plate.[6] First, the name of the game as an associate at a top law firm is billable hours (and as you get more senior, chargeable hours or hours that will be billed to a client without discount). Generally, the more projects you are working on, the more potential billable hours it is possible to generate. Assuming the work is available, it is a good idea to distinguish yourself from peers by exceeding both the minimum hours required by the firm and the minimum hours required to be eligible for a bonus, assuming there are multiple targets. Second, at times you will want to put one project down for a bit, perhaps to think things through before finishing or because the partner is reviewing it to confirm that you are on the right track. At those times, it helps to have a lot of other assignments you can work on. Lastly, if other partners notice that you are someone their fellow partners trust with their client matters, they are likely to follow suit.

Pro Bono Service

In addition to billable matters and assuming you have satisfied your requirement for minimum hours, consider adding to your plate a pro bono project. Providing pro bono work allows you to serve the public good and may help you obtain hands-on experience early on perhaps in a whole new area of practice that you might not receive otherwise. However, understand that your firm may not provide billable credit for hours spent on pro bono work. Hence, fill your plate with billable matters first. Then, if you decide to take on pro bono work, write a memorandum to the appropriate firm person in an effort to get the time to count as "billable credit" for bonus and other purposes. Even if the firm ultimately denies the request, you have on record that you were working some hours pro bono.

Communicate Time Commitments

Another component of managing work effectively is to communicate time commitments. In line with the advice to keep a full plate, it is helpful to communicate time commitments without saying no, if possible. Thus, if a partner asks for help on a project and you are filled up, explain that you want to help, ask about the timing of her project, and let her know about any time-sensitive matters currently on your plate. Proceeding in this way

---

6. For advice on budgeting and organizing your time, see John Sapp, Making Partner: A Guide for Law Firm Associates 27–32 (American Bar Association, 3rd ed. 2006).

may keep you in the running for the project, because not every project has to be completed tomorrow or yesterday. After providing all the information and getting a sense of the partner's deadline for the new project, determine, with the partner's input, whether you could feasibly handle the project. Given the goal of keeping a full plate, you may want to err on the side of taking on the new project—assuming either that the project is not time sensitive or that you do not have more time-sensitive projects than you can handle.

Follow Through

A third component of managing work effectively is to follow through on your commitments. Maintaining a full plate is important, but you do not want to overpromise by taking on too much work or providing a deadline that could be too ambitious in an effort to please the partners.

Obviously, all associates start out intending to follow through and to meet deadlines. So this part is really about knowing your limits. What is the maximum amount, or types, of projects you can handle simultaneously without compromising on deadlines previously promised? This limit will vary from person to person, so even though a partner thinks you should be able to handle a certain amount, it does not necessarily mean you can—or, even if you can, that your performance will not be affected. Also keep in mind that the time budgeted for the project is relevant but not determinative. You may not want to bill for more than the time allotted, but it may still take you longer than that time to complete.

To help ensure that you follow through on your commitments, consider (1) overestimating the time it will take you to complete a particular project; and (2) informing the partner before a deadline if there is a chance you will not complete a project when promised.

Overestimate Your Timing

At first your limit may be difficult to assess, because it depends so heavily on how accurately you estimate the time required to complete each project. Thus, you may want to give yourself a little more of a time cushion (perhaps an additional day) than you think you need. Generally the projects will take longer than you think, particularly because you are a junior associate learning the substantive law as well as how to satisfy the partner's stylistic preferences. Once you have this cushion, however, be careful to not fall into the pattern many lawyers follow—filling the time you have for a project just because you can. With experience you will become more adept at gauging your timing, and overestimating will not be necessary.

Communicate Potential Timing Delays

When you receive an assignment, consider not promising to complete the project by a certain date other than the partner's deadline, if one is provided. What if you do promise to complete a project by a certain date, and you cannot perform or you cannot meet the partner's deadline? Be sure to give the partner advance notice that you will not be able to comply, along with a reasonable explanation. For example, you are close to getting to the bottom of an issue you researched (and if the partner is interested, here is the result of your analysis to date) but need a little more time to confirm your current thinking.

Depending on the project, the partner may appreciate your keeping him or her apprised of your status and potential timing delay and you can buy some needed breathing room as far as a revised due date. Regardless, this practice is important, because you certainly do not want the reputation around the firm or in your group that you are one who promises but does not deliver.

ACCORDING TO TOP LAW FIRM SENIOR PARTNERS:
Communicating Time Commitments
- "Give me a realistic view of your workload. Don't promise what you can't deliver."
- "The best associate will regularly keep me informed of the status of his/her "plate.""

Follow Through
- "Fulfill commitments. In other words, do what you say you are going to do when you say you are going to do it."
- "I do place the full burden on the associate to tell me as soon as possible if a deadline is unrealistic; if I disagree, we can discuss. If 'perfect' is not possible by the deadline, the deadline is unrealistic (but may be binding if it's the client's deadline)."
- "Keep me informed. If you don't think that you are going to meet the deadline or you run into problems, let me know sooner rather than later."

SOFT SKILL 4: SEEK SPECIFIC FEEDBACK AND TAKE ACTION

A fourth key to being a top performer at a top law firm is to seek specific feedback on a regular basis and take immediate action to improve in the areas identified for growth and development.

Law school typically does not teach you how to be a stellar associate, so you are likely to benefit from regular, constructive feedback from partners. The feedback can range from how to be a more effective lawyer generally to fundamentals to work on specifically. Possible areas to discuss, for example, are soft skills 1 through 3 of this chapter: Are you communicating consistently with partner preferences? Are you rigorous in your legal research and writing? Are you effectively managing your workload?

Seek Specific Feedback Regularly

To execute this soft skill, do not wait until your scheduled annual or semi-annual performance review to seek feedback. Instead, request at least one or two meetings in between those scheduled reviews with the partners with whom you are working. Solicit their opinions about how you are doing, and find out what areas could use improvement. Partners (and later, outside clients) will appreciate the opportunity to provide feedback, and the process can only help you become a stronger lawyer.

For the meeting, prepare ahead by sending the partner specific questions you have to ensure that the topics you want addressed are covered. Here are some possible areas to ask about for any particular project: (1) Did you talk like a lawyer by conveying information persuasively in a clear, concise, and logical manner? (2) Did you think like a lawyer by demonstrating strong analytical and reasoning skills in evaluating the substantive issue? (3) What were the merits of the conclusions you reached? (4) Did you write like a lawyer by being rigorous, organized, and concise? (5) Did you take a reasonable amount of time to finish the project? You can also ask about your performance more globally as opposed to on a particular project. For example, find out whether your knowledge and understanding of the fundamental principles of the area of law in which you are working is sufficient.

Be open to all comments, even if you do not agree, and try not to take anything personally.

Take Immediate Action

Once issue areas are identified, ask for specific suggestions needed to improve in a particular area if none were provided or you are unsure how to take corrective measures. Then make it clear that you appreciate the partner's taking time to give you feedback and say that you intend to develop a plan for improvement in these areas. Shortly after the meeting, develop and send a plan of action to the partner. Then, set up a follow-up appointment to assess your progress before the next scheduled formal review.

You can follow this same approach of seeking specific feedback by preparing ahead of time and taking action to improve when the time comes for your regularly scheduled annual or semiannual review.

SOFT SKILL 5: MAKE OTHERS LOOK GOOD

A fifth key to being a top performer at a top law firm is to make others look good. Everyone wants credit for performing well or having a good idea. However, the most successful associates relish their role as the supporting cast, or "backbenchers,"[7] and let others shine.

Relish Your Role as Support

There will be plenty of time later to be in the limelight. For now, however, as a junior associate, recognize and appreciate your role, which is to help make partners look good and provide them all the necessary tools for that purpose (research, memoranda, talking points, organizing files, etc.). Part of your responsibility here is to make sure you understand how the partner prefers to be supported in various settings before, during, and after the event (conference calls, client meetings, e-mails, etc.). For example, does the partner want you to prepare a follow-up memorandum to be sent to the partner for forwarding to the client? As you can gather, not all the work or the projects will be glamorous. Regardless, do not be so anxious to get on a client call or meet with the client. Instead, perform your role as supporting cast to the best of your ability, and you will have plenty of chances to "sit up front" later.

Let Others Take Credit

A top performer does not take credit for working hard, getting to the bottom of an issue, or proposing original ideas. She knows that extra effort is

---

7. A backbencher is a member of the British Parliament or a similar legislative body who is not a party leader and individually does not have much power to influence government policy. However, backbenchers are important in providing services to their constituents and in relaying the opinions of their constituents.

expected in the process of trying to obtain the best result for the client, so she does not deserve or expect special recognition. Moreover, the top performer recognizes that if there is an opportunity to take credit, that credit should be shared with others whenever possible. Following are examples of letting partners and associates take credit.

Partners

A smart associate at a top law firm understands that generally it is the partner who is to be seen and heard, not the associate. Thus the associate is mindful of his place on conference calls and in client meetings with the partner.

So, if a brilliant idea comes to you on a client conference call in which you are participating, communicate the idea to the partner off-line rather than saying the idea out loud. He can then decide whether the idea has merit and, if so, present it as his own. If the idea has some legs, you may get credit from the partner that can be just as important as impressing the client. Remember that for all intents and purposes, the partner is your client. If the idea has no merit, at least you have not embarrassed the partner or yourself.

Another way to make a partner look good is to provide him current articles or newspaper stories you come across that may be of interest to a firm client. The partner can decide whether he wants to forward the piece to the client, who likely will perceive that the partner was thinking about him and his matters—a very good thing.

Associates

Making your associate colleagues look good is also important. You are all a team; so to the extent a colleague is helpful to you on a project, it is important to share credit. If an associate has a brilliant idea or helps solve a problem, be sure to brag about her to the partner and not necessarily in her presence.

SOFT SKILL 6: DOCUMENT PERFORMANCE RESULTS ANNUALLY

A sixth key to being a top performer at a top law firm is to summarize your yearly performance statistics and successes in the form of a memorandum to firm management. Many associates will not follow this advice, believing instead that their excellent work will speak for itself so the memorandum is not necessary. But if you are a star, then why not make your case for receiving the maximum bonus and highest salary increase available to you?

Prepare Comprehensive Memorandum

Firm management may not know you other than your numbers, so they likely will appreciate your effort in the form of a thoughtful, well-written memorandum making your case. A written memo demonstrates that your performance is important to you and worthy of management's consideration. The memorandum should be clear, persuasive, and to the point. Include the following information: (1) firm statistics for the year; (2) intangible accomplishments; and (3) comparable firm data. Also discussed here are the steps surrounding the transmittal of the memorandum and ideas for following up.

Provide Firm Statistics for the Year

The law firm is most interested in measures of your productivity. What is the amount of revenue you brought in for the year? More specifically, provide detail about how many hours you billed, how many of those hours were written off, how many of those hours were collected, total amount of collections, and expected collections coming after the memorandum is presented, and so on. In addition, provide detail about the top three matters, measured by billable hours, for which you worked, including hours spent and whether you expect those matters to continue into the following performance year. You also may want to provide information concerning where generally you expect your hours to come from in the following year. This is helpful information for management, and it demonstrates that you are firm focused and understand the business side of practicing law.

List Intangible Accomplishments

In addition to the numbers, did you accomplish anything specifically worth mentioning? If so, provide that information. Consider the following: achieving successful result for a client; attracting a new client or a potential new client; achieving success in a pro bono matter; publishing an article; presenting at a bar or other conferences; earning recognition relating to involvement in firm activities such as the summer associate program, or mentoring, and spending time helping with partner responsibilities such as billing, recruiting, and developing a business plan.

Include Comparable Firm Data

Take nothing for granted in this process. If you want your memorandum to be persuasive concerning the appropriate level of bonus and salary given your performance, you have to do the work to demonstrate what a comparable firm would pay you based on your level and experience. One of the keys is to make sure the information you provide is for firms that are comparable to your firm. For example, if you work for a satellite office of a St. Louis firm in Washington, D.C., it may not be relevant that an associate at your level at a D.C.-based firm is earning more. Instead, a comparable firm likely would have a medium-sized office in D.C. and be based in a city where the cost of living is about the same as in St. Louis.

So, look for firms in the AmLaw 100 that are similarly situated—first in terms of home office and then in terms of profitability. Use the AmLaw 100 metrics of gross revenue, profit per partner, and revenue per lawyer to pick ten or so comparable firms. Compile the most current information available about comparable law firms regarding bonus, billable hour requirements, and salary for each associate year. This information is on various websites, but obviously it is important to make sure the information is current or disclose that it is not. You may also be able to confirm the accuracy of some of the data with help from an interested legal recruiter.

Then, prepare an Excel spreadsheet listing the firms including your firm, the different metrics, and the salary and bonus amounts offered. Next, compute an average which seems like a reasonable way to account for outliers of these amounts and enter that number on the spreadsheet and in the memorandum. Finally, using the firm's typical verbiage, make a soft request to be paid at least that average amount. For example, "I understand my firm is committed to attracting and retaining the top talent in this market."

Transmitting the Memo and Follow-up

The next step is to transmit the memorandum and follow-up. This step involves the following three parts as discussed below: (1) follow the chain of command, (2) make your case orally as well, and (3) ask the firm to reconsider if you are unhappy with the result.

Follow the Chain of Command

Find out from the partner with whom you work most closely what is appropriate when requesting a salary increase, including who should be involved, and follow that approach. This practice is important, so that feathers do not get ruffled and so that you can incorporate various comments in the memorandum and prepare a stronger argument. You do not want to shoot yourself in the foot by sending your request to the wrong people or not sending it to someone who should have been included. If you are in a practice group, the protocol may be to send the memorandum to your practice group leader. He or she then forwards it to someone higher up in firm management. If you are sending the request to several recipients, be mindful of the order you list them on e-mail, because some people will care.

Send the memorandum with plenty of time to have it reviewed up the chain of command before salary and bonus decisions are made. When asking someone to review the memorandum, be sensitive to that partner's busy schedule. Notify him or her that you are planning on summarizing your performance for your year-end review, and ask when it would be helpful to have that document so that you can incorporate comments in time. The person reviewing could be someone in the chain of people who will receive the memorandum, which is probably a good idea if he or she is willing.

Make Your Case Orally as Well

A good time to make your case is during your evaluation period. You should make your case orally to the partner with whom you work most closely and anyone else whom the partner suggests (i.e., a partner in firm management, a partner who participates in your evaluation meeting), so that you can highlight the points in the memorandum that you want the firm to focus on. This step is crucial because partners may not have a chance to read your memorandum, much less focus on parts that are important to you.

Ask for Reconsideration

If you are unhappy with the result and the poor or nonexistent explanation that followed, consider asking for reconsideration. It shows seriousness of purpose, and it is not the end of the world if the firm denies your request or tells you no twice. Depending on the facts, this may be time for you to start looking for another job. But before jumping ship, it may be helpful to understand management's rationale if one exists. Perhaps no one received raises, for example.

SOFT SKILL 7: HAVE A PARTNER MIND-SET

A seventh key to being a top performer at a top law firm is to have a partner mind-set. If you have any interest in making partner, it will help you to start thinking and acting like a partner from the beginning. Obviously, partner activity varies at different law firms and by partner. In general, however, partners wear suits even though the firm has a casual dress code, focus on the firm when it comes to decision making, prioritize business development, and are committed to maximizing client service. These items are discussed in more detail next. To the extent possible, follow the lead of these partners. Partners may take notice of you and be more inclined to assign work to you; but more important, you increase your chances of success as a junior associate by acting as if within appropriate boundaries you have already made it to the next level.

Dress Code

Having a partner mind-set includes dressing the part. As discussed, jackets and ties and dressy suits seem to be optional at many top law firms these days. Nevertheless, some partners, usually the rainmaker types, continue to wear suits daily. Follow the example of those partners lead if your goal is to make partner. When you dress the part, both partners and clients tend to take you more seriously. Many associates make partner without dressing up, but dressing well is just one more way to differentiate you from the rest of the associates with high numbers who produce good work and also want to make partner.

Firm-Focused Decisions

Having a partner mind-set includes having a firm focus when it comes to decision making. That means thinking about day-to-day choices based on how they affect the firm and its partners, not just you personally. Two reasonable places to consult in an effort to make decisions that are firm centric are the firm's policy manual and its mission statement. The firm's mission statement likely will give you a good idea about what the firm stands for, the firm's reason for existing, and its values. When making a decision, ask yourself whether what you are doing is consistent with the firm's mission. For example, suppose your firm's mission statement includes goals such as "performing legal work in a timely manner." In that case, obsessing about making your memorandum perfect at the expense of missing your deadline would be inconsistent with the firm's emphasis on timeliness.

Your actual case may not be so obvious, so if you are unsure, check with a partner. This step demonstrates awareness of the firm's mission and your conscientiousness about not wanting to make a decision that potentially could contradict firm principles.

Another place to consult is the firm's policy manual. That document generally covers a wide variety of topics relevant to a junior associate's daily choices. Some examples include the firm policy on (1) office dating; (2) using firm letterhead; (3) reimbursements for bar registration, professional memberships, continuing legal education, or other expenses such as travel; (4) outside employment; and (5) preparing correspondence, memoranda, and legal documents. You can confirm that you are taking the right approach by following the manual. If the manual does not cover your issue, you can demonstrate your firm focus by communicating to firm management that you consulted the document first and did not find guidance for your question.

Business Development

Having a partner mind-set also includes constantly thinking about ways to develop business. Inside the firm, for example, you should spend some time, even as a junior associate, on making business development a priority. Write articles, perhaps with senior partners as coauthors, and volunteer to help with client pitches. Outside the firm, make it a point to keep in regular contact with law school and college classmates and colleagues at the law firm who leave to go to other firms or to either in-house or government positions. In addition, plan to regularly attend conferences, bar association meetings, community group activities, sports activities, and events where potential clients will attend. Make the most of these events by developing a system to track your contacts and the frequency of your outreach, and communicate regularly.

Client-Focused Decisions

Having a partner mind-set includes a focus on maximizing client service. For a junior associate, the client generally is a firm partner. Three ways to maximize your service to the partner-client are to (1) respond to requests quickly, (2) take the partner's temperature regularly, and (3) add value at no additional cost.

Be Responsive

Partners appreciate quick responses to their e-mails or calls. They want to know that the message has been received, and they probably want the answer quickly too. Demonstrate that they are the priority by acknowledging as soon as you can that you have received their e-mail or phone message and you are on the case. It is probably best not to wait to respond until you have the answer, because the partner has no way of knowing if the message was received and if you are indeed working on a solution.

Take Partner's Temperature Regularly

From time to time, check in with the partner to see how he is doing and whether you are satisfying his preferences. Ask if you can be doing anything else on the projects you have worked on, or on other matters for which they may need assistance. Also keep the partner updated on the status of any outstanding items on your plate.

Add Value on Your Own Time

One appropriate way to act as if you have made it to the next level is to come up with additional ways to add value to the firm and its clients at no additional cost. For the firm, consider making a presentation for the firm's practice group on a timely subject that you have thoroughly researched. This way, multiple lawyers will have the benefit of your hard work while you demonstrate that you are a firm-focused team player.

On the client side, set out on your own time to learn everything you can about the business of your partner's clients. This activity will help you provide more effective client service. Start by reviewing the company website and then set up Google Alerts on the client. Next, keep current with news stories, articles, and federal and state legislative developments that may affect the client, and alert the partner when you find something relevant. Other ideas for adding value without billing include preparing written summaries of the (1) progress and status of open matters, (2) talking points in advance of meetings, and (3) meeting takeaways and plans for moving forward after meetings. Keep track of all your time, because some partners will be comfortable with billing every minute. Either way, providing the option for these kinds of activities should promote plenty of goodwill with the partner and ultimately with the client.

SOFT SKILL 8: SECURE AN EFFECTIVE SPONSOR

The eighth and final key to being a top performer at a top law firm is to secure an effective sponsor. This discussion considers the characteristics of a strong sponsor, the purpose of having one, and how to maximize the relationship. The takeaway here is to quickly identify a dependable sponsor with whom you get along, because that person can be helpful to you throughout your law firm career.

Characteristics

A sponsor is generally a senior partner practicing in your area. That person has ample business, and he or she is interested in teaching you the tricks of the trade and speaking up for you when helpful, including when it comes time to deciding who to make partner. Ideally, the sponsor is someone who carries a lot of weight in the firm, either directly by being in firm management or indirectly by generating enough revenue to be influential. This quality is important because you need not only a champion, but a champion with some pull.

Purpose

At a top law firm, a sponsor is helpful to have when you are an associate. The sponsor mentors you, and makes sure your plate is always full. A sponsor is also crucial to have once you make partner, and you are in the transition period of not being an associate but not having enough of your own clients to generate sufficient billable work to keep you busy. That period could last anywhere from three to five years or longer, depending on your ability to generate business. During this period, you may find that once the cases you are working conclude, other partners are not anxious to assign you more work when they can assign that work to associates with lower billing rates and thereby avoid the consternation of a client who would notice multiple partners on the monthly invoices. This reality is yet another reason to have a sponsor, one who sticks around until you make partner and then for your entire transition period. Perhaps he can even groom you to take over some or all of his practice and then you will be in very good shape.

Maximize Relationships

Schedule coffee every couple of weeks to meet with your sponsor, even if he or she is also the partner who assigns most of your work projects. During these meetings, discuss day-to-day and big-picture items to get feedback and confirm you are on the right track. For example, review your current projects and perhaps get into the weeds if the sponsor is amenable; your deadlines; the people with whom you are working, including partners you are getting to know; and your participation in firm and other activities (e.g., speaking, writing, bar association panels or events, etc.). On the big-picture side, make sure that you are exceeding or at least meeting expectations for your associate level with regards to substantive work, soft skills, and participation in firm and outside activities. If not, ask for specific suggestions for improvement.

Now that you have become a top-perfroming associate in part by following the soft skill practices provided above, you have moved a long way toward your goal of making partner. Executing the action steps discussed in Chapter 5 will take you even closer.

CHAPTER 5

How to Make Partner at a Top Law Firm

TAP 5: To become a partner:

1. Stay productive.
2. Be actively involved inside and outside the firm.
3. Serve in leadership roles in the firm.
4. Demonstrate that you care about the business of practicing law.
5. Become an expert.
6. Consider secondment opportunities.
7. Make your case.

This chapter provides examples of some finishing touches that will help the productive associate advance on the fast track to partner.

First, do good work and continue to perform at the highest levels by exceeding minimum billing requirements, and making sure partners are collecting on your time. Second, be actively involved inside and outside the firm by participating in firm leadership roles, including mentoring younger lawyers. Next, demonstrate that you care about the business of practicing law by helping with the billing process, from reviewing the invoice to dealing with clients who have questions. Round out your candidacy by becoming an expert. In addition, consider working in-house for a prominent firm client for a couple of years as a way of gaining high-level, substantive training. Finally, discuss your prospects with the appropriate lawyer and, assuming you are being considered, make your case in a formal memorandum for why you deserve admittance into the partnership.[1]

STAY PRODUCTIVE

Maintain a consistent pattern of producing good work and generating high billings that are substantially collected. As discussed in earlier chapters, satisfying partner preferences, managing your workload effectively, and securing an effective sponsor who can help ensure that you have a full plate should all be helpful in this regard. In addition, to stay continually busy, reach out from time to time to partners other than those with whom you primarily work. Also, become known around your practice group as the go-to person for certain projects that no one claims. Take on these projects even if the subject matter is not the most interesting. It will be helpful to have an area that everyone recognizes as yours, so that you have a monopoly on those projects.

BE ACTIVELY INVOLVED INSIDE THE FIRM

Participate regularly in firm activities, such as committees (associates, diversity, social, etc.) and summer associate functions. Serve in various firm leadership roles. You can get involved in many types of firm activities. For example, consider serving as the coordinator for the monthly (or whenever) meetings of your practice group. As leader, you can make your imprint by inviting relevant guest speakers to discuss the hot topics in your practice area. You can have different lawyers present material on a timely topic, or you can have participants briefly summarize their projects. People in firm management are likely to take notice anytime you take on a leadership role in the firm. Another leadership role you could try is the head of the associates committee, who represents the group in dealing with firm management. Here too you can make your imprint with guest speakers and other bold ideas not commonly undertaken in the law firm setting. Of course you want to be careful not to be too bold and sabotage your partnership chances. A third leadership role you could try is participating in the summer associate program as a mentor to one of the summer associates.

---

1. One little-known secret of top firms is that the complement of skills that help someone first to become a top-performing associate and later to be considered for partner are not necessarily the same skills that help someone become a top-performing partner. There is some overlap; but some of the items to focus on as a partner, such as actively seeking referrals and raising your profile, are less important as an associate. Chapter 6 discusses these and other items required for success as a junior partner.

BE ACTIVELY INVOLVED OUTSIDE THE FIRM

Outside the firm, seek leadership positions in bar associations. Also, join industry organizations in which your clients belong, attend the meetings, and read the industry publications your clients read. If it is appropriate to help develop your practice, be active in your community, perhaps through your church or temple or some other forum that could lead to potential client contacts.

DEMONSTRATE THAT YOU CARE ABOUT THE BUSINESS OF PRACTICING LAW

You can become cognizant of the business side of law practice in at least three ways: (1) seek supervisory responsibility over client matters; (2) seek to become the point person for a client's bill; and (3) review statistical reports that you have access to (presumably at least your billings, collections, charge-offs, etc.) as well as new business reports.

Seek Supervisory Responsibility

One way to demonstrate interest in learning the business of practicing law is to seek supervisory responsibility over several matters. This means that in addition to mentoring younger associates and giving them feedback on their work, you are in charge of staffing the project, preparing project estimates for clients, and attending to many aspects of client management. These duties include reviewing and sending out the client bills and, in some cases when the relationship partner cedes control, answering client questions about the bills.

As a supervising lawyer, one of your tasks is to ensure that a project is properly staffed with the appropriate lawyers so that work is completed efficiently and consistent with client timing. With practice, you will learn to keep fees down by using leveraging: have younger associates perform the research and prepare the memoranda before you pitch in to help them refine their analysis. In many cases, toward the end of the project, it may make sense for you to involve a partner presumably the relationship partner who can help confirm conclusions reached and offer general, big-picture observations to further refine the work product provided to the client.

Seek to Become Point Person for Client Bills

Another way to demonstrate interest in learning the business of practicing law is to seek greater exposure to one of the partner's clients by volunteering to become the point person for the bills. This may not be the most glamorous role, but it will give you a crash course in the business side. For example, you may have to handle client complaints about the total size of the bill or explain the hours you or other lawyers spent on certain projects.

When dealing with the client who is questioning certain fees, the key is to be deferential while standing behind the fees charged. Toward that end, give the client all of the information necessary to answer the factual question, including what work was done, the general amount of time it takes someone of that level to do that work, and any other information pertinent to the question. This process may involve at least two calls—one call to find out the nature of the inquiry and then a follow-up call after you have collected the relevant information and given a heads-up to the billing partner so you understand the latitude you have in resolving the question. It is not usually a good idea to say no, or that the firm cannot do what the client wants, no matter how outrageous the client's request may seem (i.e., cut the bill in half). Use discretion, of course; but depending on your discussion with the partner, you may be in a position where you can tell the client that you will recommend that the firm or the billing partner make some adjustments to meet the client halfway or less and explain that you will confirm and report back. Generally, the client likes to feel that you have given in on at least one of the issues raised no matter how insignificant. Creation of goodwill, or potential destruction of goodwill, could turn out to be important for a sustainable, long-term relationship and future bill discussions when it may be acceptable to give less or nothing, given the reasonableness you have shown this time.

Review Statistical and New Business Reports

A third way to demonstrate interest in learning the business of practicing law is to review and become familiar with firm statistical reports and the new business report. Even as an associate, you likely will have access to your statistical information such as total billings, collections, charge-offs, and the like. You probably also will have access to some statistical information of fellow associates and perhaps partners (i.e., hours billed). Having this information helps you document your yearly performance results and determine where you stand vis-à-vis your colleagues. Knowing the bottom line (the extent of revenue you generate minus your costs) is ultimately what matters, because law firms are a business. Your mentor should be able to guide you as to appropriate revenue targets for your associate level.

In addition to taking an interest in the statistical information, show the firm that you care about the business by reviewing the "new business" report, which describes all the new files opened in the preceding time period. If you notice one of the partners in your group has opened a new file, go and ask her about the project and let her know you are available to help if needed.

BECOME AN EXPERT

Create a name for yourself in a particular sub-specialty within your practice group. Perhaps it is a sub-specialty you find interesting, or perhaps it is one that has been relevant to several of your earlier projects. For example, appoint yourself as the litigation lawyer who focuses on asbestos litigation or the tax lawyer who focuses on planning involving Subchapter S corporations. Consult with your sponsor about possible sub-niche areas that could be beneficial for you and the firm. Then, start a blog at your firm covering the sub-niche you picked.

To help develop your expertise, take continuing legal education courses on the subject. Also develop your brand by speaking and writing about the sub-niche area for which you chose to focus. To ensure that your speaking or writing skills are at the highest possible level, consider taking a speaking and/or writing course. For litigators, for example, the National Institute for Trial Advocacy hosts conferences that help participants perfect their oral advocacy and writing skills. Talk with your sponsor, and have him or her assess your writing and speaking skills and provide feedback generally (concerning what you could improve) and specifically (concerning the specific article or speech for which you are working). While developing your sub-niche, you may also want to consider writing an article with your sponsor or another established partner at the firm as a coauthor.

To maximize your results, be particular about the places you choose to present speeches and the publications for which you choose to write. You want to target places accessible to potential clients who will be interested in your services and able to afford your billing rate. You also should have a goal of pursuing events and publications where you would stand out.

Speaking on an American Bar Association panel is good experience, but speaking to a room full of lawyers in your practice area is not likely to generate new clients. Instead, consider attending and presenting at a client seminar or a trade conference in your sub-niche area. These events are likely to include few lawyers, so you will have an immediate advantage.

Moreover, firm clients and potential clients will recognize that you are becoming an expert.

Similarly, writing articles for legal publications is good experience, but writing for trade publications about your sub-niche could be especially beneficial in getting you exposure among nonlawyers. For example, within the real estate practice group, you can focus on hospitality and then target trade publications dealing with hospitality. You could also contribute to client bulletins and newsletters.

CONSIDER SECONDMENT

Consider possible secondment opportunities. Secondment occurs when a law firm temporarily loans one of its lawyers to a client to work in-house, in exchange for a fixed or reduced rate. The experience has many benefits including the hands-on opportunity to deal directly with clients on interesting matters and the chance to expedite your evolution from a junior technical lawyer into an effective legal and business counselor.

Secondment seems like a win-win situation for the associate and the firm in general, because it opens up opportunities for both parties during the arrangement and after the secondment has concluded. Once the secondment is finished, if you decide to stay with the client, perhaps this decision can strengthen the relationship between the top law firm and the client. Alternatively, if you decide to return to the firm, you are much more marketable to that client and other clients. This reputation helps you to make your case for partner.[2]

MAKE YOUR CASE

The next step is to make your case in writing and orally, notwithstanding the fact that neither of these measures may be required by the firm.

In Writing
Prepare an extensive memorandum documenting all your years of service and all your accomplishments both statistically (hours billed and collected) and substantively (notable wins for various clients). The memorandum will summarize the key points of your year-end performance submissions. It also will present your argument stating why you are ready to represent

---

2. Craighton Goeppele, *Second This! A Personal Look Back at My Secondment*, ABA BUSINESS LAW SECTION (January/February 2008), available at http://apps.americanbar.org/buslaw/blt/2008-01-02/goeppele.shtml (last visited July 11, 2013).

the firm as a partner. For this second piece, consult any firm materials that describe qualifications for partnership and then address each one in the memorandum. In addition to these items, provide a short summary of your business plan with goals, and detail how you intend to generate new clients for the firm either in your sub-niche area or another area.[3] Ask the partners with whom you work and your sponsor to review your memorandum.

As is the case with the annual performance memoranda, this document will assist the firm decision makers who may not know you other than your numbers. A written product demonstrates that making partner is important to you and that your admission to the firm is worthy of management's consideration.

Orally

Ask for the opportunity to make your case for admission orally. If the request is granted, you can highlight the points in the memorandum for which you want the firm to focus. This step is vital because partners may not have a chance to read your memorandum, much less focus on the parts that are important to you.

Now that you have taken the action steps above and transitioned from star associate to partner at a top law firm, it is time to consider how to become a top performing junior partner. Chapter 6 discusses the action steps necessary to accomplish that objective.

---

3. For assistance with this effort, see LINDA PINSON, THE LAWYER'S GUIDE TO CREATING A BUSINESS PLAN: A STEP-BY-STEP SOFTWARE PACKAGE, 2012 EDITION CD-ROM (ABA Law Practice Management Section, May 2012).

CHAPTER 6

How to Succeed as a Junior Partner at a Top Law Firm

TAP 6: To succeed as a junior partner:

1. Manage current clients effectively.
2. Network strategically.
3. Actively seek referrals.
4. Have the long view.
5. Continue to build your brand and distinguish yourself.

This chapter provides advice about specific actions to take, and a mind-set to have, to succeed as a junior partner at a top law firm. Also included at the end of the chapter is advice from senior partners at top law firms about how to build a strong practice.

Some find the transition from star associate to low-level partner difficult. Perhaps that explains why few people who start as an associate at a top firm will make partner and continue with the firm. For example, to make partner, you must produce consistently high-quality work and meet higher and higher goals for billable hours. If you are on track, your rate gets higher each year. Thus, by the time you make partner, the partners who previously turned to you for help are looking to the younger associates with lower rates to work on their matters. That leaves you in a bit of a bind. Now it is time to focus on client development, assuming you have the temperament. Even if you do have some ability in this area, developing clients takes time and requires patience. This reality explains why the previous chapters emphasize developing a partner mind-set early and stress the importance of becoming an expert in a sub-specialty and raising your profile.

The key to success as a junior partner is to stay busy by continuing to perform the steps and exhibit the soft skills that allowed you to make partner long enough to build a practice. For example, you have to manage current clients effectively so they are regularly informed and feel important. Likewise, to be a top-performing associate, you have to satisfy partner preferences so they are constantly updated and feel as if they are your first priority. As another example, to succeed as a junior partner, you have to continue to build your brand and distinguish yourself, perhaps by leaving the firm for a short time to gain technical or hands-on experience in government or industry. This step is comparable to and a continuation of your path to make partner, which involved establishing your expertise in a sub-niche by speaking frequently on the topic at industry group conferences and writing for their publications.

This chapter builds upon guidance previously provided by adding advice about how to maintain the long view and how to network strategically and seek referrals. To be successful, the junior partner must be patient and committed to spending the time necessary to build a practice. At the same time, you must stay productive by convincing fellow partners to continue to use you and benefit from your sub-niche expertise, notwithstanding your higher billable rate. Successful junior partners follow this approach because they understand that the business development cycle is ongoing. For some prospective clients, it takes one meeting; for others, it takes a year or perhaps several years to secure the engagement.

The following sections offer specific advice on how to (1) manage current clients effectively; (2) network strategically; (3) seek referrals from clients, colleagues, and friends; (4) maintain the long view; and (5) continue to build your brand and distinguish yourself.

MANAGE CURRENT CLIENTS EFFECTIVELY

In general, when dealing with clients you can apply the same approach you use for dealing with partners, as discussed earlier. The two keys to effective client management are to maintain regular contact and make the client feel special whenever possible.

Like partners when you were an associate, clients want to feel as though they are your first priority. So, at a minimum, return all calls and e-mails soon after receiving them. And generally keep the client informed of the status of his project on a regular basis, even if you have nothing significant to report. In addition, schedule regular calls (weekly, biweekly, etc.) to discuss anything on the client's mind, including whether legal needs are being adequately met.

Clients also appreciate seeing their lawyers go above and beyond what is required as part of the engagement. As a start, learn the client's business on your own time. In addition, keep abreast of the current and potential issues facing the client's industry. Scan relevant periodicals and news stories for articles that may be of interest to the client. Set up an automatic news e-mail alert, so that you are notified about various federal and state legislative and regulatory actions that potentially could affect the client. Do not bill any of this time.

NETWORK STRATEGICALLY

Learning to network strategically is important as a partner because your time will continue to be limited. Billable requirements at top law firms do not disappear once you become partner. They may be reduced, but for the most part you have to stay billable for six to eight hours per day. Thus, much of your time will be spent networking internally with partners to make sure you have a steady flow of work until your business starts booming. For all these reasons, you have to be strategic about your client development time. Try not to chase so-called dogs, small matters, or matters that are likely never to materialize.

One example of networking strategically is to have regular (every week, every two weeks) meetings with a new prospect or someone (another partner, a friend, an acquaintance with good contacts) who may be able to connect you with a new prospect. You can meet for lunch; some people say that you should never eat alone.[1] Or, meeting in the morning for coffee may work better. Suggesting an early time shows sensitivity to the prospect's busy schedule and may mean less chance they will cancel.

Another example of networking strategically is to limit your participation in outside conferences or meetings where many lawyers with your background are searching for business. For example, a tax lawyer would be wasting her time attending tax section meetings for the purpose of securing client leads. However, that lawyer would be well served to attend bond association conferences, where fewer tax lawyers are present and thus she faces less competition.

---

1. KEITH FERRAZZI, NEVER EAT ALONE: AND OTHER SECRETS TO SUCCESS, ONE RELATIONSHIP AT A TIME (Doubleday, 2005).

A third example of networking strategically is to attend cocktail parties that potential clients may attend. At a party, refrain from consuming the food and drinks. If you focus on stuffing your face with appetizers and getting free drinks, you will have less time for meaningful conversations with many prospects. Instead, keep your eye on the ball, which is to obtain contacts for following up purposes. Water is okay to drink and carry; you can use it for removing yourself from a conversation with someone who does not seem like a good prospect, because you can finish quickly and walk away to refill.

A couple of other tips to maximize your results are to come early and develop a system for remembering names. Be the person who greets the first couple of guests as they arrive. It will give you something to talk about and put you in the chatting mood. You also want to make sure to connect with many people in a short period of time. When talking with people, use their name as often as possible to help you remember their name and position yourself to establish a sincere relationship with that person. As Dale Carnegie says, the sweetest sound to anyone's ear is the sound of their own name.[2]

Along the lines of meeting lots of prospects, do not overstay in any conversation even if it is going well. You should generally try to leave people wanting more, so get what you need as far as contact information and a follow-up item and then move on to the next person. Also take notes about the interaction with each person in real time. Right after you meet a new person, take two minutes to write three facts about that person on the back of his or her card. For example, jot down one physical characteristic and two other facts that you may be able to use when following up.

You should also consider refraining from attending a dinner if one happens to follow the cocktail hour, because dinner is generally not very productive. You really only have two opportunities to meet someone (the people to your left and right) and even if one of them is a potential prospect, your conversation is usually interrupted by speeches given at the dinner. Moreover, after all the talking you did during the cocktail hour, you will not likely be in the mood to sit through a two-hour dinner. So, instead go home and work on how you will follow up with the prospects you met during the cocktail hour.

---

2. DALE CARNEGIE, HOW TO WIN FRIENDS AND INFLUENCE PEOPLE (Simon & Schuster, 1981).

ACTIVELY SEEK REFERRALS

From Existing Clients

Referrals can come from various sources, including existing clients. You can increase the likelihood that they will come from existing firm clients by doing good work and following up with clients when the project is complete. The follow-up could include a so-called postmortem meeting, either by telephone or in person, during which you ask whether the client was pleased with the result, including the timing and the cost. If the client is pleased, it is a natural time to ask, if the client is comfortable, whether he would consider recommending you to others based on his positive experience.

From Colleagues

You can take at least two steps and increase the chances of getting referrals from colleagues. First, make sure the partners at the firm know your particular expertise by regularly communicating by e-mail or orally a short summary of your specific experience and recent successes in the area.

Next, review the firm's client list to determine whether any clients could benefit from knowing about a certain successful result you achieved. Then, target the billing partners on those matters with your e-mails. You are likely to secure some decent work projects for firm clients by using this process.

From Friends

To increase the chances that referrals come from friends, follow an approach similar to that used for colleagues. Make a list of 50 people you know who are successful now, or who you think will be successful in the future, and stay in contact with them. When reaching out, ask how you can be helpful other than providing legal services. Perhaps you can connect your friend with a client of the firm or someone else you know who can be helpful for their business. As with your partners, make sure your friends are aware of your particular expertise by regularly communicating a short summary of your specific experience and recent successes in the area. Stay in constant contact, and you likely will secure at least one client from this group.

HAVE THE LONG VIEW

One of the keys to success as a junior partner involved in client development is patience, or having the long view. Some prospective clients become actual clients with no effort at all from you, and some require years of nurturing. The difficult part is that everyone is different; timing and circumstances also matter, so it is best not to seek signposts and certainty where none exist. It ultimately comes down to the question of how much effort you are willing to put toward each prospect while understanding that all your effort could be a waste of time notwithstanding the learning experience from failing and how you can improve your approach.

Also, and perhaps most important, is the question of how long you can sustain yourself with other partners' projects until you bring in the big client or clients. The best situation would be if a rainmaker partner you work with was close to retiring. In that case, you may be able to inherit her clients or at least secure billable hours until your prospects come through. Securing an effective sponsor, as discussed previously, could help you through this transition period.

Do not be discouraged if you do not see results soon enough. You never know what is happening behind the scenes. The day when you are thinking nothing is happening could be the day you land the next big client for the firm. Moreover, sometimes the clients who generate the most significant projects in terms of billings start out with very small projects, so keep that in mind if the clients you are attracting initially are not bringing in significant revenue in the beginning.

CONTINUE TO BUILD YOUR BRAND AND DISTINGUISH YOURSELF

Chapter 5 emphasized the importance of building your brand by becoming an expert in a sub-niche as you pursue admission to the partnership. In the year or two after you make partner, the objective is to continue speaking and writing frequently while staying productive and building a practice by managing current clients effectively, networking strategically, and seeking referrals from various sources. At the end of your second year as partner, with an eye toward the long view, it may make sense for you to gain experience outside the firm in an effort to further build your brand and distinguish yourself.

One step that can make you more valuable from a client's perspective is to leave the firm for a stint in a government position. Doing so can beef up your technical bona fides and help further demonstrate your expertise in your sub-niche. For example, if your sub-niche is international tax law, consider working as a staffer for a tax committee on Capitol Hill. By learning how the government approaches a particular problem and understanding the policy considerations underlying certain statutes, you can better serve firm clients when you return.

These days, it is common for both associates and partners to leave firms for government positions. The concept is called the revolving door, and it refers to leaving private practice and going to government and then returning to private practice at your original firm or another firm. No promises are made on either side about returning, but in any event it is helpful for the firm to have lawyers leave for prestigious government positions.

Another step that can make you more valuable is to leave the firm for an opportunity in the business world. For example, if your sub-niche is hospitality law, you may consider becoming or working for a developer. This experience should allow you to better serve firm clients should you return by helping them anticipate and avoid many of the same pitfalls you encountered when you were in the business.

As a way to stand out from the competition, consider leaving and gaining additional experience even if everything is going well. Note, however, that it may not make sense for you to leave the firm, particularly right after you make partner, which could be viewed as poor form. If you continue to stay productive while honing your skills, focusing on your sub-niche, and landing your own clients, it may make sense to stay. Seek feedback from your mentor and fellow partners about whether to leave, optimal timing, and opportunities you may not have considered.

Many partners could provide valuable suggestions about which places to investigate and perhaps help connect you with a decision maker in those places. When approaching your mentor or other partners, demonstrate that you have a thoughtful approach by articulating the reasons your move to a certain government position or somewhere else could help the firm in the long term. For example, if the firm has a thriving tax practice but does not have a strong presence in tax lobbying, your move to the Hill and subsequent return could help the firm attract clients in that area.

Always have a long view, and communicate that view even if you currently believe you will not return to the firm. You never know what will happen, and you could be missing out on some valuable assistance for getting to that next step now.

ACCORDING TO AMLAW 100 FIRM SENIOR PARTNERS, BUILDING A STRONG PRACTICE REQUIRES THE FOLLOWING:

- "Fundamentally, a solid law practice is built on the clients' belief in the lawyer's abilities, focus and caring about the clients and their businesses. I believe the three stages of becoming a good lawyer are: (1) learning the law and legal analysis; (2) learning legal economics; and (3) learning client management. The most important component of a strong practice is gaining an understanding of each client's business objectives and concerns, so that your advice can be considered practical rather than theoretical, and so that the client can believe that you understand and appreciate his/her business and assessment of business risk."

- "Although there is no pat answer, I would say that it takes at least 10 years of hard work to build a strong practice. Mentoring is therefore a critical element of success, because the time and difficulty involved in business development is otherwise very discouraging to most."

- "Always return calls and e-mails promptly. Keep clients informed. Do not be condescending. Ask the client what he/she thinks. Make an effort to learn the client's business off the clock. Give the client reasons to believe you care about him/her that will resonate with the client. Make yourself something other than a major expense to the client."

- "The measure of a rainmaker and top lawyer is how he or she performs under duress and difficulty. If you're not busy enough, take time to learn more about the businesses you represent, or take another state bar or qualify for a specialty certification. Sit in on a piece of complex business litigation to learn the consequences of poor planning and advice in the boardroom. Whatever you do, don't panic! Your peers are concerned about the same things you are, and you can achieve a substantial advantage simply by having and executing on a plan."

CONCLUSION

Consistent with the notion that repetition is helpful and generally necessary when writing like a lawyer, this conclusion attempts to distill all of the advice provided in the chapters above together into three clear-cut steps.

To achieve success in law school, land a top law firm job, and excel once there, take the following action steps: 1) choose a practice area and build your expertise, 2) network strategically with a broad brush, and 3) practice persistence together with a long view mindset. These steps form an iterative process such that implementing each of them with refinements along the way can be helpful throughout one's law career. For best results, apply these steps after you have determined that you are comfortable pursuing a position at a top law firm, despite the sales skills required at each stage as described in chapter 2.

For example, chapter 1 emphasizes the importance of picking a law major and chapters 5 and 6 discuss the importance of specializing within a practice area. Choosing an appealing practice area early (and taking courses in that field) will help you (i) succeed in law school because one tends to perform well if interested in the subject matter; (ii) secure a position with a top law firm because employers are interested in candidates that have demonstrated a commitment to a particular area of law; (iii) become a top-performing associate because you will be able to both work on demonstrating substantive proficiency in your area of focus and refine some of the soft skills discussed such as satisfying partner preferences and securing an effective sponsor with the partners in your practice area; (iv) make partner because you will be able to develop a niche expertise within your practice area; and (v) succeed as a junior partner because you will be able to continue to build your brand and distinguish yourself.

Similarly, chapters 1, 3, and 6 emphasize the value of networking with different people depending on your purpose (i.e., professors, alumni, friends, senior associates, partners, and clients). Networking strategically with a broad brush will help you (i) succeed in law school because the people with whom you meet will help you determine your area of focus with the result that targeted course selection and strong academic performance will follow; (ii) secure a position with a top law firm because you will connect with people who care that you have distinguished yourself; (iii) become a top-performing associate because you will be able to determine partner preferences in part by reaching out to other associates and partners; (iv) make partner because you will be engaged with people inside and outside the firm; and (v) succeed as a junior partner because you will seek referrals from partners and clients.

Lastly, chapters 4 and 6 emphasize the significance of practicing persistence. Practicing persistence in conjunction with taking the long view will help you (i) succeed in law school because you will not be deterred by one or two subpar grades or by the time-consuming, rigorous process required to determine your "major;" (ii) secure a position with a top law firm because you will not be discouraged by constant rejection; (iii) become a top performing associate because you will not be dissuaded by working with difficult partners, navigating though complex legal issues which may not have clear answers, or receiving insufficient or zero feedback from partners; (iv) make partner because you will not be disheartened if you do not make partner when first eligible and you will continue trying; and (v) succeed as a junior partner because you will understand that some prospective clients take years of nurturing such that you need to continue to put forth effort and not be dejected when clients do not engage you right away.

I hope you found the guidance in this book helpful, and straightforward to follow along the way to achieving a rewarding legal career.
